John Kendrick Bangs

Toppleton's Client

A Spirit in Exile

John Kendrick Bangs

Toppleton's Client
A Spirit in Exile

ISBN/EAN: 9783743357068

Manufactured in Europe, USA, Canada, Australia, Japa

Cover: Foto ©ninafisch / pixelio.de

Manufactured and distributed by brebook publishing software (www.brebook.com)

John Kendrick Bangs

Toppleton's Client

TOPPLETON'S CLIENT

OR

A SPIRIT IN EXILE

BY

JOHN KENDRICK BANGS

LONDON
JAMES R. OSGOOD, McILVAINE & CO.
45, ALBEMARLE STREET, W.
1893

[All rights reserved]

TO
F. D. S.

CONTENTS.

CHAPTER I.
INTRODUCING MR. HOPKINS TOPPLETON . . . 1

CHAPTER II.
MR. HOPKINS TOPPLETON LEASES AN OFFICE . 13

CHAPTER III.
MR. HOPKINS TOPPLETON ENCOUNTERS A WEARY SPIRIT 25

CHAPTER IV.
THE WEARY SPIRIT GIVES SOME ACCOUNT OF HIMSELF 39

CHAPTER V.
HOPKINS BECOMES BETTER ACQUAINTED WITH THE WEARY SPIRIT 55

CHAPTER VI.
THE SPIRIT UNFOLDS A HORRID TALE . . 73

CHAPTER VII.
A CHAPTER OF PROFIT AND LOSS . . 90

CHAPTER VIII.

FURTHER DEVELOPMENTS IN THE MAKING OF A NAME 107

CHAPTER IX.

THE CROWNING ACT OF INFAMY 124

CHAPTER X.

THE SPIRIT'S STORY IS CONCLUDED . . . 149

CHAPTER XI.

TOPPLETON CONSULTS THE LAW AND FORMS AN OPINION 167

CHAPTER XII.

TOPPLETON MAKES A FAIR START . . . 184

CHAPTER XIII.

AT BARNCASTLE HALL 201

CHAPTER XIV.

THE DINNER AND ITS RESULT 218

CHAPTER XV.

BARNCASTLE CONFIDES IN HOPKINS . . . 232

CHAPTER XVI.

MR. HOPKINS TOPPLETON MAKES A DISCOVERY 251

CHAPTER XVII.

EPILOGUE 268

TOPPLETON'S CLIENT.

CHAPTER I.

INTRODUCING MR. HOPKINS TOPPLETON.

MR. HOPKINS TOPPLETON, Barrister, of London and New York, was considered by his intimates a most fortunate young man. He was accounted the happy possessor of an income of something over fifty thousand dollars a year, derived from investments which time had shown to be as far removed from instability, and as little influenced by the fluctuations of the stock market, as the pyramids of Egypt themselves. Better than this, however, better even than personal beauty, with which he was plentifully endowed, Mr. Hopkins Toppleton was blessed with a great name, which he had received ready-made from his illustrious father, late head of the legal firm of Toppleton, Morley, Harkins, Perkins, Mawson, Bronson, Smithers and Hicks. The value of the name to Hopkins was unquestionable, since it enabled him, at his father's death, to enter that famous aggregation of legal talent as a special partner, although his knowledge of law was scant, receiving a share of the profits of the concern for the use of his patronymic, which, owing to his father's pre-eminent success at the Bar, Messrs. Morley, Harkins, *et al.*, were anxious to retain. This desire of Mr. Toppleton's late associates was most natural, for such was the tremendous force exerted by the name he bore, that plaintiffs when they perceived it arrayed in opposition to their claims, not infrequently withdrew their suits, or offered terms upon which any defendant of sense might be induced to compromise. On the other hand, when a defendant found himself confronted with the fact that Hopkins Toppleton, Sen., had joined forces with the plaintiff, he usually either settled the claim against him in full or placed himself beyond the jurisdiction of the courts.

When Toppleton, Sen., died, it was very generally believed that the firm, whose name has already been mentioned at some length, lost not only its head, but also a very large proportion of its brains,—a situation quite as logical as it was unfortunate for the gentlemen with whom Mr. Toppleton had been associated.

Nor was this feeling, that with the departure of Toppleton, the illustrious, for other worlds the firm was deprived of a most considerable portion of its claims to high standing, confined to cavilling outsiders. No one recognized the unhappy state of affairs at the busy office on Broadway more quickly than did Messrs. Morley, Harkins, Perkins, Mawson, Bronson, Smithers, and Hicks themselves, and at the first meeting of the firm, after the funeral of their dead partner, these gentlemen unanimously resolved that something must be done.

It was at this meeting that Mr. Hicks suggested that the only course left for the bereaved firm to pursue, if it desired to remain an aggressive force in its chosen profession, was to retain the name of Toppleton at the masthead, and, as Mr. Mawson put it, "to bluff it out." Mr. Perkins agreed with Mr. Hicks, and suggested that the only honest way to do this was to induce Mr. Toppleton's only son, known to all—even to the clerks in the office—as Hoppy, to enter the firm as a full partner.

"I do not think," Mr. Perkins said, "that it is quite proper for us to assume a virtue that we do not possess, and while Hoppy—I should say Hopkins—has never studied law, I think he could be induced to do so, in which event he could be taken in here, and we should have a perfectly equitable claim to all the business which the name of Toppleton would certainly bring to us."

"I am afraid," Mr. Bronson put in at this point, "I am very much afraid that such a course would require the entire reorganization of the firm's machinery. It would never do for the member whose name stands at the head of our partnership designation, to be on such terms of intimacy with the office boys, for instance, as to permit of his being addressed by them as Hoppy; nor would it conduce toward good discipline, I am convinced, for the nominal head of the concern to be engaged in making pools on baseball games with our book-keepers and clerks, which, during his lamented father's life, I understand was one of the lad's most cherished customs. Now, while I agree with my friend Perkins that it is desirable that the firm should have an unassailable basis for its retention of the name of Toppleton, I do not agree with him that young Hopkins should be taken in here if we are to retain our present highly efficient force of subordinates. They would be utterly demoralized in less than a month."

"But what do you suggest as an alternative?" inquired Mr. Morley.

"I believe that we should make Hopkins a

special partner in the firm, and have him travel abroad for his health," returned Mr. Bronson after a moment's reflection.

"I regret to say," objected Mr. Hicks, "that Hoppy's health is distressingly good. Your point in regard to the probable demoralization of our office force, however, is well taken. Hopkins must go abroad if he becomes one of us; but I suggest that instead of sending him for his health, we establish a London branch office, and put him in charge on a salary of, say, 10,000 dollars. We have no business interests outside of this country, so that such a course, in view of his absolute ignorance of law, would be perfectly safe, and we could give Hoppy to understand in the event of his acceptance of our proposition that he shall be free to take a vacation whenever he pleases, for as long a period of time as he pleases, and the oftener the better."

"That's the best plan, I think," said Mr. Mawson. "In fact, if Hoppy declines that responsible office, I wouldn't mind taking it myself."

And so it happened. The proposition was made to Hopkins, and he accepted it with alacrity. He did not care for the practice of the law, but he had no objection to receiving an extra ten thousand dollars a year as a silent partner in a flourishing concern with headquarters in London, particularly when his sole duties were to remain away from the office on a perpetual vacation.

"I was born with a love of rest," Hoppy once said in talking over his prospects with his friends some time before the proposition of his father's partners had been submitted to him. "Even as a baby I was fond of it. I remember my mother saying that I slept for nearly the whole of my first year of existence, and when I came to my school days my reputation with my teachers was, that in the enjoyment of recess and in assiduous devotion to all that pertained to a life of elegant leisure, there was not a boy in school who could approach me."

The young man never railed at fate for compelling him to lead a life which would have filled others of robuster ideas with ennui, but he did on occasions find fault with the powers for having condemned him to birth in a country like the United States, where the man of leisure is regarded with less of reverence than of derision.

"It is a no harder fate for the soul of an artist to dwell in the body of a pork-packer," he had said only the night before the plan outlined by Mr. Hicks was brought to his attention, "than for a man of my restful tendencies to be at home in a land where the hustler alone inspires respect. What the fates should have done in my case was clearly to have had me born a rich duke or a prince, whose chief duty it would be to lead the fashionable world and to set styles of dress for others to follow. I'd have made a magnificent member of the House of Lords, or proprietor of a rich estate somewhere in England, with nothing to do but to spend my income and open horse shows; but in New York there is no leisure class of recognized standing, excepting, of course, the messenger-boys and the plumbers, and even they do not command the respect which foreign do-nothings inspire. It's hard luck. The only redeeming feature of the case is that owing to a high tariff I can spend my money with less effort here than I could abroad."

Then came the proposition from the firm, and in it Hoppy recognized the ingredients of the ideal life—a life of rest in a country capable of understanding the value to society of the drones, a life free from responsibility, yet possessing a semblance of dignity bound to impress those unacquainted with the real state of affairs. Added to this was the encouragement which an extra ten thousand a year must invariably bring to the man appointed to receive it.

"It's just what I needed," he said to Mr.

Hicks, "to make my income what it ought to be. Fifty thousand dollars is, of course, a handsome return from investments, but it is an awkward sum to spend. It doesn't divide up well. But sixty thousand a year is simply ideal. Twelve goes into sixty five times, and none over—five thousand a month means something, and doesn't complicate accounts. Besides, the increase will pay the interest on a yacht nicely."

"You are a great boy, Hoppy," said Mr. Hicks, when the young man had thus unbosomed himself, "but I doubt if you will ever be a great man."

"Oh, I don't know," said Hoppy; "there's no telling what may develop. Of course, Mr. Hicks, I shall go into the study of the law very seriously; I couldn't think of accepting your offer without making some effort to show that I deserved it. I shall give up the reading of my irresponsible days, and take to reading law. I shall stop my subscription to the sporting papers, and take the *Daily Register* and *Court Calendar* instead, and if you think it would be worth while I might also subscribe to the *Albany Law Journal*, with which interesting periodical I am already tolerably familiar, having kept my father's files in order for some years."

"No, Hoppy," said Mr. Hicks, with a smile, "I don't think you'd better give up the sporting papers; 'all work and no play makes Jack a dull boy.'"

"Perhaps you are right," said Hopkins, in reply to this. "But I *shall* read Blackstone, and accumulate a library on legal subjects, Mr. Hicks. In that I am firm. I am a good deal of a book-lover anyhow, and since law is to be my profession I might as well suit my books to my needs. I'll order a first edition of Blackstone at once."

"You'd better get the comic Blackstone," said Mr. Hicks, gravely. "You will find it a very interesting book."

"Very well, Mr. Hicks," returned the amiable head-partner-elect of the famous legal firm, "I'll make a note of that. I will also purchase the 'Newgate Calendar,' and any other books you may choose to recommend, —and I tell you what, Mr. Hicks, when my collection gets going it will be the talk of the town. I'll have 'em all in absolute firsts, and as for the bindings, your old yellow-backed tomes at the office will be cast utterly in the shade by my full crushed levant morocco books in rich reds and blues. Just think of the hundred or more volumes of New York reports in Russia leather, Mr. Hicks!"

"It takes my breath away, Hoppy," returned the lawyer. "Every one of the volumes will be absolutely uncut, I suppose, eh?"

"Never you mind about that," retorted Hopkins; "you think I'm joking, but you'll find your mistake some day. I'm serious in this business, though I think I'll begin my labours by taking a winter at Nice."

"That is wise," said Mr. Hicks, approvingly; "and then you might put in the summer in Norway, devoting the spring and autumn to rest and quiet."

"I'll think about that," Hopkins answered; "but the first step to take, really, is to pack up my things here, and sail for London and secure an office."

"A very proper sentiment, my dear boy," returned Mr. Hicks; "but let me advise you, do not be rash about plunging into the professional vortex. Remember that at present your knowledge of the law is limited entirely to your theories as to what it ought to be, and law is seldom that; nor must you forget that in asking you to represent us in London, it is not our desire to inflict upon you any really active work. We simply desire you to live in an atmosphere that, to one of your tastes, is necessarily broadening, and if you find it advisable to pursue intellectual breadth across the continent of Europe to the uttermost parts of the earth, you will find that the firm stands ready to furnish you with material assistance, and to remove all obstacles from your path."

"Thanks for your kindness, Mr. Hicks," said Hopkins. "I shall endeavour to prove myself worthy of it."

"I have no doubt of it, my boy," rejoined Mr. Hicks, rising. "And, in parting with you, let me impress upon you the importance, both to you and to ourselves in the present stage of your legal development, of the maxim, that to a young lawyer not sure of his law, and devoid of experience, there is nothing quite so dangerous as a client. Avoid clients, Hoppy, as you would dangerous explosives. Many a young lawyer has seemed great until fate has thrown a client athwart his path."

With these words, designed quite as much for the protection of the firm, as for the edification of that concern's new head, Mr. Hicks withdrew, and Hopkins turned his attention to preparations for depature; paying his bills, laying in a stock of cigars, and instructing his valet as to the disposition of his lares and penates. Four weeks later he sailed for London, arriving there in good shape early in

June, ready for all the delights of the season, then at its height.

It was not until Hopkins had been four days at sea, that the firm of Toppleton, Morley, Harkins, Perkins, Mawson, Bronson, Smithers, and Hicks learned that the new partner had presided at a Coney Island banquet, given by himself to the office-boys, clerks, book-keepers, and stenographers of the firm, on the Saturday half-holiday previous to his departure. It is doubtful if this appalling fact would have come to light even then, had not Mr. Mawson, in endeavouring to discharge one of the office-boys for insubordination, been informed by the delinquent that he defied him; the senior member of the firm, the departed Hoppy, having promised to retain the youth in his employ at increased wages, until he was old enough to go to London, and assist him in looking after the interests of his clients abroad. An investigation, which followed, showed that Hopkins had celebrated his departure in the manner indicated, and also divulged the interesting fact that the running expenses of the office, according to the new partner's promises, were immediately to be increased at least twenty-five per cent. per annum in salaries.

CHAPTER II.

MR. HOPKINS TOPPLETON LEASES AN OFFICE.

IT did not take Hopkins many days to discover that a life of elegant leisure in London approximates labour of the hardest sort. Nor was it entirely easy for him to spend his one thousand pounds a month, with lodgings for his headquarters. This fact annoyed him considerably, for he valued money only for what it could bring him, and yet how else to live than in lodgings he could not decide. Hotel life he abhorred, not only because he considered its excellence purely superficial, but also because it brought him in contact with what he called his "flash-light fellow countrymen, with Wagnerian voices and frontier manners"—by which I presume he meant the diamond studded individuals who travel on Cook's Tickets, and whose so-called Americanism is based on the notion that Britons are still weeping over the events of '76, and who love to send patriotic allusions to the star-spangled banner echoing down through the corridors of the hotels, out and along the Thames Embankment, to the very doors of parliament itself.

"Why don't you buy a house-boat?" asked one of his cronies, to whom he had confided his belief that luxurious ease was hard on the constitution. "Then you can run off up the Thames, and loaf away the tedious hours of your leisure."

"That's an idea worth considering," he replied, "and perhaps I'll try it on next summer. I do not feel this year, however, that I ought to desert London, considering the responsibilities of my position."

"What are you talking about?" said the other with a laugh. "Responsibilities! Why, man, you haven't been to your office since you arrived."

"No," returned Hoppy, "I haven't. In fact I haven't got an office to 'be to.' That's what bothers me so like thunder. I've looked at plenty of offices advertised as for rent for legal firms, but I'll be hanged if I can find anything suitable. Your barristers over here have not as good accommodations as we give obsolete papers at home. Our pigeon-holes are palatial in comparison with your office suites, and accustomed as I am to breathing fresh air, I really can't stand the atmosphere I have been compelled to take into my lungs in the rooms I have looked at."

"But, my dear fellow, what more than a pigeon-hole do you need?" asked his friend. "You are not called upon to attend to any business here. A post-office box would suffice for the receipt of communications from America."

"That's all true enough," returned Hopkins, "but where am I to keep my law library? And what am I to do in case I should have a client?"

"Keep your books in your lodgings, and don't count your clients before they get into litigation," replied the other.

"My dear Tutterson," Hopkins said in answer to this, "you are the queerest mixture of common sense and idiotcy I have ever encountered. My library at home, indeed! Haven't you any better sense than to suggest my carrying my profession into my home life? Do you suppose I want to be reminded at every step I take that I am a lawyer? Must my business be rammed down my throat at all hours? Am I never to have relaxation from office cares? Indeed, I'll not have a suggestion of law within a mile of my lodgings! I must have an office; but now that I think of it, not having to go to the office from one year's end to another, it makes no difference whether it consists of the ground floor of Buckingham Palace or a rear cell three flights up, in Newgate Prison."

"Except," returned Tutterson, "that if you had the office at Newgate you might do more business than if you shared Buckingham Palace with the Royal family."

"Yes; and on the other hand, the society at the palace is probably more desirable than that of Newgate; so each having equal advantages, I think I'd better compromise and take an office out near the Tower," said Hopkins. "The location is quite desirable from my point of view. It would be so inaccessible that I should have a decent excuse for not going there, and besides, I reduce my chances of being embarrassed by a client to a minimum."

"That is where you are very much mistaken," said Tutterson. "If you hang your shingle out by the Tower, you will be one lawyer among a hundred Beef-Eaters, and therefore distinguished, and likely to be sought out by clients. On the other hand, if you behave like a sensible man, and take chambers in the Temple, you'll be an unknown attorney among a thousand Q.C's. And as for the decent excuse for not attending to business, you simply forget that you are no longer in America but in

England. Here a man needs an excuse for going to work. Trade is looked down upon. It is the butterfly we esteem, not the grub. A man who *will* work when he doesn't need to work, is looked upon with distrust. Society doesn't cultivate him, and the million regard him with suspicion,—and the position of both is distinctly logical. He who serves is a servant, and society looks upon him as such, and when he insists upon serving without the necessity to serve, he diminishes by just so much the opportunities of some poor devil to whom opportunity is bread and butter, which sets the poor devil against him. You do not need an excuse for neglecting business, Toppleton, and, by Jove, if it wasn't for your beastly American ideas, you'd apologize to yourself for even thinking of such a thing."

"Well, I fancy you are right," replied Toppleton. "To tell you the truth, I never thought of it in that light before. There is value in a leisure class, after all. It keeps the peach-blow humanity from competing with the earthenware, to the disadvantage of the latter. I see now why the lower and middle classes so dearly love the lords and dukes and other noble born creatures Nature has set above them. It is the generous self-denial of the aristocracy in the matter of work, and the consequent diminution of competition, that is the basis of that love. I'll do as you say, and see what I can do in the Temple. Even if a client should happen to stray in at one of those rare moments when I am on duty, I can assume a weary demeanour and tell him that I have already more work on my hands than I can accomplish with proper deference to my health, and request him to take his quarrel elsewhere."

So the question was settled. An office was taken in the Temple. Hopkins bought himself a wig and a gown, purchased a dozen tin boxes, each labelled with the hypothetical name of some supposititious client, had the room luxuriously fitted up, arranged his law library, consisting of the "Comic Blackstone," "Bench and Bar," by Sergeant Ballantyne, the "Newgate Calendar," and an absolute first of "Parsons on Contracts," on the mahogany shelves he had had constructed there; hung out a shingle announcing himself and firm as having headquarters within, and, placing beneath it a printed placard to the effect that he had gone out to lunch, he turned the key in the door and departed with Tutterson for a trip to the land of the Midnight Sun.

Now it so happened, that the agent having in charge the particular section of the Temple in which Hopkins' new office was located, had concealed from the young American the fact that for some twenty-five or thirty years, the room which Toppleton had leased had remained unoccupied—that is, it had never been occupied for any consecutive period of time during that number of years. Tenants had come but had as quickly gone. There was something about the room that no one seemed able to cope with. Luxuriously furnished or bare, it made no difference in the fortunes of Number 17, from the doors of which now projected the sign of Toppleton, Morley, Harkins, Perkins, Mawson, Bronson, Smithers, and Hicks. Just what the trouble was, the agent had not been able to determine in a manner satisfactory to himself until about a year before Hopkins happened in to negotiate with him for a four years' lease. Departing tenants, when they had spoken to him at all on the subject, had confined themselves to demands for a rebate on rents paid in advance, on the rather untenable ground that the room was uncanny and depressing.

"We can't stand it," they had said, earnestly "There must be some awful mystery connected with the room. There has been a murder, or a suicide, or some equally dreadful crime committed within its walls at some time or another."

This, of course, the agent always strenuously

denied, and his books substantiated his denial. The only possible crime divulged by the books, was thirty-three years back when an occupant departed without paying his rent, but that surely did not constitute the sort of crime that would warrant the insinuation that the room was haunted.

"And as for your statement that the room makes you feel weird and depressed," the agent had added with the suggestion of a sneer, "I am sure there is nothing in the terms of the lease which binds me to keep tenants in a natural and cheerful frame of mind. I can't help it, you know, if you get the blues or eat yourselves into a state that makes that room seem to you to be haunted."

"But," one expostulating tenant had observed, "but, my dear sir, I am given to understand that the five tenants preceding my occupancy left for precisely the same reason, that the office at times is suffocatingly weird; and that undefined whispers are to be heard playing at puss in the corner with heart-rending sighs at almost any hour of the day or night throughout the year, cannot be denied."

"Well, all I've got to say about that," was the agent's invariable reply, "is that *I* never saw a sigh or heard a whisper of a supernatural order in that room, and if you want to go to law with a case based on a Welsh rarebit diet, just do it. If the courts decide that I owe you money, and must forfeit my lease rights because you have dyspepsia, I'll turn over the whole business to you and join the army."

Of course this independent attitude of the agent always settled the question at once. His tenants, however insane they might appear to the agent's eyes, were invariably sane enough not to carry the matter to the courts, where it was hardly possible that a plaintiff could be relieved of the conditions of his contract, because his office gave him a megrim, superinduced by the visit of a disembodied sigh.

Judges are hard-headed, practical persons, who take no stock in spirits not purely liquid, realizing which the tenants of Number 17, without exception, wisely resolved to suffer in silence, invariably leaving the room, however, in a state of disuse encouraging to cobwebs, which would have delighted the soul of a connoisseur in wines.

" If I can't make the rent of the room, I can at least raise cobwebs for innkeepers to use in connection with their wine cellars," said the agent to himself with a sad chuckle, which showed that he was possessed of a certain humorous philosophy which must have been extremely consoling to him.

At the end of three years of abortive effort to keep the room rented, impelled partly by curiosity to know if anything really was the matter with the office, partly by a desire to relieve the building of the odium under which the continued emptiness of one of its apartments had placed it, the agent moved into Number 17 himself.

His tenancy lasted precisely one week, at the end of which time he moved out again. He, too, had heard the undefined whispers and disembodied sighs; he, too, had trembled with awe when the uncanny quality of the atmosphere clogged up his lungs and set his heart beating at a galloping pace; he, too, decided that so far as he was concerned life in that office was intolerable, and he acted accordingly. He departed, and from that moment No. 17 was entered on his books no longer as for rent as an office, but was transferred to the list of rooms mentioned as desirable for storage purposes.

To the agent's credit be it said that when Hopkins Toppleton came along and desired to rent the apartment for office use his first impulse was to make a clean breast of the matter, and to say to him that in his own opinion and that of others the room was haunted and had been so for many years; but when he reflected that his conscience, such as it was, along with the rest of his being, was in the employ of the proprietors of the building, he felt that it was his duty to hold his peace. Toppleton had been informed that the room was useful chiefly for storage purposes, and if he chose to use it as an office, it was his own affair. In addition to this, the agent had a vague hope that Hopkins, being an American and used to all sorts of horrible things in his native land—such as boa-constrictors on the streets, buffaloes in the back yard, and Indians swarming in the suburbs of the cities,—would be able to cope with the invisible visitant, and ultimately either subdue or drive the disembodied sigh into the spirit vale. In view of these facts, therefore, it was not surprising that when Hopkins had finally signed a four years' lease and had taken possession, the agent should give a sigh of relief, and, on his return home, inform his wife that she might treat herself to a new silk dress.

During the few weeks which elapsed between the signing of the lease and Hopkins' ostensible departure on a three months' lunching tour, he was watched with considerable interest by the agent, but, until the " Gone to Lunch " placard was put up, the latter saw no sign that Hopkins had discovered anything wrong with the office, and even then the agent thought nothing about it until the placard began to accumulate dust. Then he shook his head and silently congratulated himself that the rent had been paid a year in advance; "for," he said, "if he hasn't gone to New York to lunch, the chances are that that sigh has got to work again and frightened him into an unceremonious departure." Neither of which hypotheses was correct, for as we have already heard, Hopkins had departed for Norway.

As for the sigh, the young lawyer had heard it but once. That was when he was about leaving the room for his three months' tour, and he had attributed it to the soughing of the wind in the trees outside of his window, which was indeed an error, as he might have discovered at the time had he taken the trouble to investigate, for there were no trees outside of his window through whose branches a wind could have soughed even if it had been disposed to do so.

CHAPTER III.

MR. HOPKINS TOPPLETON ENCOUNTERS A WEARY SPIRIT.

IT was well along in October when Hopkins returned to London, and he got back to his office in the Temple none too soon. The agent had fully made up his mind that he was gone for good, and was about taking steps to remove his effects from Number 17, and gain an honest penny by sub-letting that light and airy apartment for his own benefit, a vision of profit which Toppleton redivivus effectually dispelled.

The return, for this reason, was of course a grave disappointment to Mr. Stubbs, but he rose to the occasion when the long lost lessee appeared on the scene, and welcomed him cordially.

"Good morning, sir," he said. "Glad to see you back. Didn't know what had become of you or should have forwarded your mail. Have a pleasant trip?"

"Very," said Toppleton, shortly.

"It seems to have agreed with you,—you've a finer colour than you had."

"Yes," replied Hopkins, drily. "That's natural. I've been to Norway. The sun's been working day and night, and I'm tanned."

"I hope everything is—er—everything was all right with the room, sir?" the agent then said somewhat anxiously.

"I found nothing wrong with it," said Hopkins; "did you suspect that anything was wrong there?"

"Oh, no!—indeed not. Of course not," returned the agent with some confusion. "I only asked—er—so that in case there was anything you wanted, you know, it might be attended to at once. There's nothing wrong with the room at all, sir. Nothing. Absolutely nothing."

"Well, that's good," said Toppleton, turning to his table. "I'm glad there's nothing the matter. It will take a very small percentage of the rental to remedy that. Good morning, Mr. Stubbs."

"Good morning, sir," said Mr. Stubbs, and then he departed.

"Now for the mail," said Hopkins, grasping his letter-opener, and running it deftly through the flap of a communication from Mr. Morley, written two months previously.

"Dear Hoppy," he read. "We have just been informed of your singular act on the Saturday previous to your departure for London."

"Hm! what the deuce did I do then?" said Hopkins, stroking his moustache thoughtfully. "Let me see. 'Singular act.' I've done quite a number of singular things on Saturdays, but what—Oh, yes! Ha, ha! That Coney Island dinner. Oh, bosh!—what nonsense! as if my giving the boys a feast were going to hurt the prospects of a firm like ours. By George, it'll work just the other way. It'll fill the force with an enthusiasm for work which—"

Here Hopkins stopped for a moment to say, "Come in!" Somebody had knocked, he thought. But the door remained closed.

"Come in!" he cried again.

Still there was no answer, and on walking to the door and opening it, Toppleton discovered that his ears had deceived him. There was no one there, nor was there any sign of life whatever in the hallway.

"I'm glad," he said, returning to his chair and taking up Mr. Morley's letter once more. "It might have been a client, and to a man at the head of a big firm who has never been admitted to practice in any court or country, that would be an embarrassment to say the least. It's queer though, about that knock. I certainly heard one. Maybe there is some telepathic influence between Morley and me. He usually punctuates his complaints with a whack on a table or back of a chair. That's what it must have been; but let's see what else he has to say."

"Of course," he read, "if you desire to associate with those who are socially and professionally your inferiors, we have nothing to say. That is a matter entirely beyond our jurisdiction, but when you commit the firm to outrageous expenditures simply to gratify your own love of generosity, it is time to call a halt."

"What the devil is he talking about?" said Hopkins, putting the letter down. "I paid for that dinner out of my own pocket, and never charged the firm a cent, even though it does indirectly reap all the benefits. I'll have to write Morley and call his attention to that fact. How vulgar these disputes—"

At this point he was again interrupted by a sound which, in describing it afterwards, he likened to a ton of aspirates sliding down a coal chute.

"This room appears to be an asylum for strange noises," said he, looking about him to discover, if possible, whence this second interruption came. " I don't believe Morley feels badly enough about my behaviour for one of his sighs to cross the ocean and greet my ears, but I'm hanged if I know how else to account for it, unless there's a speaking tube with a whistle in it somewhere hereabouts. I wonder if that's what Stubbs meant!" he added, reflecting.

"Bah!" he said in answer to his own question, picking up Mr. Morley's letter for a third time. "This is the nineteenth century. Weird sounds are mortal-made these days, and I'm not afraid of them. If there were anything supernatural about them, why didn't the air get blue, and where's my cold chill and my hair standing erect? I fancy I'll retain my composure until the symptoms are a little more strongly developed."

Here he returned to his reading.

" We desire to have you explain to us, at your earliest convenience," the letter went on to say, "why you have so extravagantly raised the salary of every man, woman and child in our employ, utterly regardless of merit, and without consultation with those with whom you have been associated, to such a figure that the firm has been compelled to reduce its autumn dividend to meet the requirements of the pay roll. Your probable answer will be, I presume,—knowing your extraordinary resources in the matter of explanations—that you cannot consent to be a mere figure-head, and that you considered it your duty to impress upon our clerks the fact that you are not what they might suspect under the circumstances, but a vital, moving force in the concern; but you may as well spare yourself the trouble of making any such explanation, since it will not be satisfactory either to myself or to the other members of the firm, with the possible exception of our friend Mawson, who, with his customary about-town manners, is disposed to make light of the matter. We desire to have you distinctly understand that your duties are to be confined entirely to the London office, and to add that were it not for your esteemed father's sake we should at once cancel our agreement with you. The name you bear, honoured as it is in our profession, is of great value to us: but it is, after all, a luxury rather than a necessity, and in these hard times we are strongly inclined to dispense with luxuries whenever we find them too expensive for our pockets."

Hopkins paused in his reading and pursed his lips to give a long, low whistle, a sound which was frozen *in transitu*, for the lips were no sooner pursed than there came from a far corner the very sound that he had intended to utter.

For the first time in his life Toppleton knew what fear was; for the first time since he was a boy, when he wore it that way, did he become conscious that his hair stood upon end. His blood seemed to congeal in his veins, and his heart for a moment ceased to beat, and then, as if desirous of making up for lost time, began to thump against his ribs at lightning pace and with such force that Hopkins feared it might break the crystal of the watch which he carried in the upper left-hand pocket of his vest.

Mr. Morley's letter fluttered from his nerveless hand to the floor, and, despite its severity, was forgotten before it touched the handsome rug beneath Hopkins' table. The new sensation—the sensation of fear—had taken possession of his whole being, and, for an instant, he was as one paralyzed. Then, recovering his powers of motion, he whirled about in his revolving chair and started to his feet as if he had been shot.

"This is unbearable!" he cried, glancing nervously about the room. "It's bad enough to have an office-boy who whistles, but when you get the whistle in the abstract without the advantage of the office-boy, it is too much."

Then Hopkins rang the bell and summoned the janitor.

"Tell the agent I want to see him," he said when that worthy appeared, and then, returning to his desk, he sat down and mechanically opened a copy of the *Daily Register* and tried to read it.

"It's no use," he cried in a moment, crumpling the paper into a ball and throwing it across the room. "That vile whistle has regularly knocked me out."

The paper ball reached the door just as the agent entered, and struck him athwart the watch chain.

"Beg pardon," said Hopkins, "I didn't mean that for you. Everything here seems to be bewitched this morning, that dull compilation of legal woe included."

"It's of no consequence, sir, I assure you," returned the agent uneasily.

"No, I don't think it amounts to a row of beans to a man who hates trouble," said Hopkins, referring more to the journal than to the untoward act of the paper ball. "But I say, Mr. Stubbs, I've been having a devil of a time in this room this morning, and when I say devil I mean devil."

Stubbs paled visibly. The moment he had feared had come.

"Wh—wh—what sus—seems to b—be the m—mum—matter, sir?" he stammered.

"Nothing seems, something *is* the matter," returned Hopkins. "I don't wonder you stammer. You'd stammer worse if you had been here with me three minutes ago. Stubbs, I believe this room is haunted!"

Mr. Stubbs's efforts at surprise at this point were painful to witness.

"Haunted, sir?" he said.

"Yes, haunted!" retorted Hopkins; "and by a confoundedly impertinent something or other that not only sighs and knocks on the door but whistles, Stubbs—actually whistles. Has this room a history?"

"Well, a sort of a one," returned Stubbs; "but I never heard any one complain about it on the score of whistling, sir."

"Stubbs, I believe you are lying. Hasn't somebody killed an office-boy in this apartment, for whistling?" queried Hopkins, gazing sternly at the shuffling agent.

"I'll take an affidavit that nothing of the kind ever happened," returned the agent, gaining confidence.

"That won't be necessary," said Toppleton. "I am satisfied with your assurance. But,

Stubbs, to what do you attribute these beastly disturbances? Ghosts?"

"Of course not, Mr. Toppleton," replied Mr. Stubbs. "I fancy you must have heard some boy whistling in the hall."

"How about the knock and the sigh?" demanded the American.

"The knock is easily accounted for," returned the agent. "Somebody in the room above you must have dropped something on the floor, while the sigh was probably the wind blowing through the key-hole."

"Or a bit of fog coming down the chimney, eh, Stubbs?" put in Hopkins, satirically.

"No, sir," replied poor Stubbs, growing red where he had been white; "there is no fog to-day, sir."

"True, Stubbs; and you will likewise observe there is no wind to sough through key-holes," retorted Hopkins, severely, rising and walking to the window.

Stubbs stood motionless, without an answer. Toppleton had cornered him in a flimsy pretext, and then came the climax to his horrible experience.

From behind him in the corner whence had come the sigh and the whistle, there now proceeded a smothered laugh—a sound which curdled his blood and left him so limp that he staggered to the mantel and grasped it to keep himself from falling to the floor.

Hopkins turned upon him, his face livid with anger, and the two men gazed at each other in silence for a moment, the one endeavouring to master his fear, the other to smother his wrath.

"Do you mean to insult me, Mr. Stubbs, by laughing in my face when I send for you to request explanations as to the conduct—as to the—er—the conduct of your room? It sounds ridiculous to say that, but there is no other way to put it, for it *is* the conduct of the room of which I complain. What do you mean by your ill-timed levity?"

"I pass you my word, Mr. Toppleton, I will swear to you, sir, that nothing was further from my thoughts than mirth. I agree with you that it is no laughing matter for—"

"But I heard you laugh," said Toppleton, eyeing the agent, his anger now not unmixed with awe. "You laughed as plainly as it is possible for any one to laugh, except that you endeavoured to smother the sound."

"I did nothing of the sort, Mr. Toppleton," pleaded Stubbs, his hand shaking and his eyes wandering fearsomely over toward the mysterious corner where all was still and innocent-looking. "That laugh came from other lips than mine—if, indeed, it came from lips at all, which I doubt."

"You mean," cried Toppleton, grasping Stubbs by the arm with a grip that made the agent wince, "you mean that this room is—"

"Khee-hee-hee-hee-hee!" came the derisive laugh from the corner, followed by the mysterious whistle and heartrending sigh which Hopkins had already so unpleasantly heard.

Toppleton was transfixed with terror, and the agent, with an ejaculation of fear, ran from the room, and scurried down the stairs out into the court as fast as his legs could carry him, where he fell prostrate in a paroxysm of terror.

Deserted by the agent and shut up in the room with his unwelcome visitor—for the agent had slammed the door behind him with such force that the catch had slipped and loosened the bolt, so that Toppleton was to all intents and purposes a prisoner—Hopkins exerted what little nerve force he had left, and pulled himself together again as best he could. He staggered to his table, and taking a small bottle of whiskey from the cupboard at its side, poured at least one half of its fiery contents down into his throat.

"*Similia similibus,*" said he softly to himself. "If I have to fight spirits, I shall use spirits." Then facing about, he gazed into the corner unflinchingly for a moment, following up his glance with one of the hand fire grenades that hung in a wire basket on the wall, which he hurled with all his force into the offending void. To this ebullition of heroic indignation, the only reply was a repetition of the sounds whose origin was so mysterious, but this time they proceeded directly from Toppleton's chair which stood at his side.

Another grenade, smashed into the maroon leather seat of the chair, was Hopkins' rejoinder, whereupon he was infuriated to hear the smothered laugh emanate from the depths of a treasured bit of cloisonné standing upon the mantel, within which it had been Hopkins' custom, in his apartments at home, to keep the faded leaves of the roses given to him by his friends of the fairer sex—a custom which, despite the volumes of tobacco smoke poured into the room by Hopkins and his companions night and day, kept the atmosphere thereof as sweet as a garden.

"You are a bright spirit," said Hopkins with a forced laugh. "You know mighty well that you are safe from violence there; but if you'll get out of that and give me one fair shot at you over on the washstand, you'll never haunt again."

"At last!" came the smothered voice, this

time from the top of the jar. "At last, after years of weary waiting and watching, I may speak without breaking my vow."

"Then for heaven's sake," cried Hopkins, sinking back into his chair and staring blankly at the jar, "for heaven's sake speak and explain yourself, if you do not wish to drive me to the insane asylum. Who in the name of my honoured partners are you?"

There was a moment's pause, and then the answer came,—

"I am a weary spirit—a spirit in exile—harmless and unhappy, whose unhappiness you may be able to relieve."

"I?" cried Hopkins, wildly.

"Yes, you. I am come to intrust my affairs to your hands."

"You are—"

"A client," returned the spirit.

Hopkins gasped twice, closed his eyes, clutched wildly at his heart, and slid down to the floor an inert mass.

He had fainted.

CHAPTER IV.

THE WEARY SPIRIT GIVES SOME ACCOUNT OF HIMSELF.

How long Hopkins would have remained in an unconscious state had not a cold perspiration sprung forth from his forehead, and, trickling over his temples, brought him to his senses, I cannot say. Suffice it to relate that his stupor lasted hardly more than a minute. When he opened his eyes and gazed over toward the haunted vase, he saw there the same depressing nothingness accompanied by the same soul-chilling sighs that had so discomfited him. To the ear there was something there, a something quite as perceptible to the auricular sense as if it were a living, tangible creature, but as imperceptible to the eye as that which has never existed. The presence, or whatever else it was that had entered into Toppleton's life so unceremoniously, was apparently much affected by the searching gaze which its victim directed toward it.

"Don't look at me that way, I beg of you, Mr. Toppleton," said the spirit after it had sighed a half dozen times and given an occasional nervous whistle. "I don't deserve all that your glance implies, and if you could only understand me, I think you would sympathize with me in my trials."

"I? I sympathize with you? Well, I like that," cried Toppleton, raising himself on his elbow and staring blankly at the vase. "It appears to me that I am the object of sympathy this time. What the deuce are you, anyhow? How am I to understand you, when you sit around like a maudlin void lost in a vacuum? Are you an apparition or what?"

"I am neither an apparition nor a what," returned the spirit. "I couldn't be an apparition without appearing. I suppose you might call me a limited perception; that is, I can be perceived but not seen, although I am human."

"You must be a sort of cross between a rumour and a small boy, I suppose; is that it?" queried Toppleton, with a touch of sarcasm in his tone.

"If you mean that I am half-way between things which should be seen and not heard, and other things which should be heard and not seen, I fancy your surmise approximates correctness. For my part, a love of conciseness

THE WEARY SPIRIT'S ACCOUNT OF HIMSELF. 41

leads me to set myself down as a Presence," was the spirit's answer.

"I'll give you a liberal reward," retorted Toppleton, eagerly, "if you'll place yourself in the category of an Absence as regards me and my office here; for, to tell you the truth, I am addicted more or less to heart disease, and I can't say I care to risk an association with a vocally inclined zero, such as you seem to be. What's your price?"

"You wrong me, Toppleton," returned the Presence, indignantly, floating from the edge of the vase over to the large rocking chair in the corner by the window, which began at once to sway to and fro, to the undisguised wonderment of its owner. "I am not a blackmailer, as you might see at once if you could look into my face."

"Where do you keep your face?" asked Hopkins, sitting up and embracing his knees. "If you have brought it along with you for heaven's sake trot it out. I can't ruin my eyes on you as you are now. Have you no office hours, say from ten to two, when you may be seen by those desirous of feasting their eyes upon your tangibility?"

"I am afraid you are joking, Hopkins," said the spirit, growing familiar. "If you are, I beg that you will stop. What is a good joke to some eyes is a very serious matter to others."

"That, my dear Presence," returned Toppleton, "is a very true observation, as is borne out by the large percentage of serious matter that appears in comic journals."

"Please do not be flippant," said the voice from the rocking-chair, sadly. "I have come to you as a suppliant for assistance. The fact that I have come without my body is against me, I know, but that is a circumstance over which I have absolutely no control. My body has been stolen from me, and I am at present a shapeless wanderer with nowhere to lay my head, and no head to lay there, if perchance the world held some corner that I might call my own."

"I can't see what you have to complain about on that score," said Toppleton, rising from the floor and seizing a large magnifying glass from his table and gazing searchingly through it into the chair which still rocked violently. "An individual like yourself, if you are an individual, ought to be able to find comfort anywhere. The avidity with which you have seized upon that chair, and the extraordinary vitality you seem to have imparted to its rockers, indicate to my mind that the world has about everything for you that any reasonable being can desire. If you can percolate into my apartment and make use of the luxuries I had fondly hoped were exclusively mine, I can't see what is to prevent your settling down at Windsor Castle if you will. Aren't there any comfortable chairs and beds there?"

"I don't know whether there are or not," replied the Presence. "I never went there, and being a loyal British Presence, I should hesitate very strongly before I would discommode the Royal family."

"It might be awkward, I suppose," returned Toppleton with a laugh, "if you should happen to fall asleep in the Prince of Wales' favourite arm-chair, and he should happen to come in and sit on you, for I presume you are no more visible to Royalty than you are to Republican simplicity as embodied in myself. Still, as a loyal British subject, I should think you'd rather be sat on by the Prince than by a common mortal."

As Hopkins spoke these words the chair stopped rocking, and if its attitude meant anything, its invisible occupant was leaning forward and staring with pained astonishment at the young lawyer, who was leaning gracefully against the mantelpiece. Then on a sudden the chair's attitude was relaxed and it rocked slowly backward again, resuming its former pace. A few minutes passed without a word being spoken, at the end of which time the spirit sighed deeply.

"Is there anything in this world," it asked, "is there anything too sacred for you Americans to joke about? Have you no ideals, no—"

"Plenty of ideals but no special idols," returned Hopkins, perceiving the spirit's drift. "But of course, if I hurt your feelings by joking about the Prince, I apologize. Though unasked, you are still my guest, and I should be very sorry to seem lacking in courtesy. But tell me about this body of yours. How did you come to lose it, and is it still living?"

"Yes, it is still living," replied the spirit. "Living a life of honoured ease."

"But how the deuce did you come to lose it? that's what I can't understand. I have heard of men losing pretty nearly everything but their bodies."

"As I have already told you," said the spirit, wearily, "it was stolen from me."

"And have you no clue to the thieves? Do you know where it is?"

"Yes, I know where it is. In fact I saw it only last week," replied the spirit with a sob, "and it's getting old, Toppleton, very old. When it was taken away from me it was erect of stature, broad-shouldered, muscular and full of health. To-day it is round-shouldered, flabby and generally consumptive-looking. When I occupied it, the face was clean-shaven and ruddy. The hair was of a rich auburn, the hands milk white. The carriage was graceful, and about my lips there played a smile that fascinated. The blue eyes sparkled, the teeth shone out between my lips when I smiled, like a strip of chased silver in the sunlight; I tell you, Toppleton, when I had that body it had some style about it; but now—it breaks my heart to think of it now!"

"It hasn't lost its good looks altogether, has it?" queried Hopkins, his voice slightly tremulous with the sympathy he was beginning to feel for this disembodied entity before him.

"It has," sobbed the spirit; "and I'm not surprised that it has, considering the life it has led since I lost it. The auburn hair that used to be my mother's pride, and my schoolmates' source of wit, has gradually dropped away and left a hairless scalp of an insignificant pinkish hue which would disgrace a shrimp. My once happy smile has subsided into something like a toothless sneer; for my dazzling teeth are no more. The blue eyes are expressionless, the elastic step is halting, and, what is worse, the present occupant of my physical self has grown a beard that makes me look like a pirate."

"I wonder you recognized yourself," said Hopkins.

"It was strange; but I did recognize myself by my ring which I still wear," returned the spirit. "But, Toppleton," it added, "you have no notion how terrible it is for a man to see himself growing old and breaking away from all the habits and principles of youth, powerless to interfere. For instance, my body was temperate when I was in it. I never drank more than one glass of whiskey in one day. Now it is brandy and water all day long, and it galls me, like the merry hereafter, with my temperance scruples, to see myself given over to intemperate drams. *I* never used profane language. Last Friday I heard my own lips condemn a poor unoffending fly to everlasting punishment. But I want to tell you how this outrageous thing came to pass. I want to tell you how it was that in the very bud of my existence I was robbed of a suitable case in which to go through life, and I want you, with your extraordinary knowledge of the law, as I understand it to be, to devise some scheme for my relief. If you don't, nobody will, and before many years it will be too late. The body is growing weaker every day. I can see that, and I want to get it back again before it becomes absolutely valueless. I believe that under my care, restored to its original owner, it can be fixed up and made quite respectable for its declining years. Of course the teeth and the hair are gone forever, but I think I can furbish up the smile, the eye and the hands. I know that I can restore my former good habits."

"I'm hanged if I see how I can help you," rejoined Hopkins. "Do you mean to say that the present occupant of your personality is the creature who robbed you of it?"

"Precisely," said the spirit. "He's the very same person, and, stars above us, how he has abused the premises! He has made my name famous—"

"You don't mean to say that he took your name too?" put in Hopkins incredulously.

"I mean just that," retorted the spirit. "He stole my name, my body, my prospects, my clothing—every blessed thing I had except my consciousness, and he thrust that out into a cold, unsympathetic world, to float around in invisible nebulousness for thirty long years. Oh, it is an awful tale of villainy, Toppleton! Awful!"

"You say he has made your name famous," said Toppleton. "You give him credit for that, don't you?"

"I would if the very fame accorded my name

did not tend to make me infamous in the eyes of those I hold most dear; and the beastly part of it is that I can't explain the situation to them."

"Why not?" asked Hopkins. "If you can lay all this misery bare to me, why can't you lay it before those for whose good will and admiration you are lamenting?"

"Because, Hopkins, they never address me, and it is my hard fate not to be able to open a conversation," returned the spirit. "If you will remember, it was not until you asked me who the devil I was, or some equally choice question of like import, that I began to hold converse with you; you are the only man with whom I have talked for thirty years, Hopkins, because you are the only person who has taken the initiative."

"Well, you goaded me into it," returned Hopkins. "So I can't see why you can't goad your friends of longer standing into it."

"The explanation is simple," replied the spirit. "My friends haven't had the courage to withstand the terrors of the situation. The minute I have whistled, sighed or laughed, they have made a bee line for the door, and raised such a hullabaloo about the 'supernatural visitation,' as they termed my efforts, that I couldn't do a thing with them. They've every-one of them, from my respected mother down, avoided me, even as that man Stubbs has avoided me. I believe you too would have fled if the door hadn't locked automatically, and so forced you to remain here."

"If I could have avoided this interview I should most certainly have done so," said Toppleton, candidly. "You can probably guess yourself how very unpleasant it is to be disturbed in your work by a whistle that emanates from some unseen lips, and to have your room taken possession of by an invisible being with a grievance."

"Yes, Hopkins. I've had almost the same experience myself," replied the spirit; "and to be as candid with you as you have been with me, I will say that it was just that experience, and nothing else, that is responsible for my present difficulties.

"That's encouraging for me," said Hopkins, nervously. "But tell me how have you become infamously famous?"

"The bandit who now occupies my being has violated every principle of religion and politics that he found in me when he took possession," returned the spirit, leaving the rocking-chair and settling down on the mantelpiece, in front of the clock. "Where I was a pronounced Tory he has made me vote with the

E

Liberals. Notwithstanding the fact that I was brought up in the Church of England, he joined first the dissenters and is now a thorough agnostic, and signs my name to the most outrageous views on social and moral subjects you ever heard advanced. My family have cut loose from me as I am represented by him, and the dearest friend of my youth never mentions my name save in terms of severest reprehension. Would you like that, Hopkins Toppleton?"

"I'd be precious far from liking it," Hopkins answered. "It seems to me I'd commit suicide under such circumstances. Have you thought of that?"

"Often," replied the spirit; "but the question has always been, how?"

"Take poison! Shoot yourself! Drown yourself!"

"I can't take poison. That fiend who robbed me has my stomach, so what could I put the poison into?" retorted the spirit. "Shoot myself? How? I haven't a pistol. If I had a pistol I couldn't fire it, because I've nothing to pull the trigger with. If I had something to pull the trigger with, what should I fire at? I have no brains to blow out, no heart to shoot at. I'd simply fire into air."

"How about the third method?" queried Toppleton.

"Drowning?" asked the unhappy Presence. "That wouldn't work. I've nothing to drown. If I could get under water, I'd bubble right up again, so you see it's useless. Besides, it's only the body that dies, not the spirit. You see the shape I'm left in."

"No," returned Hopkins, "I perceive the lack of shape you are left in, and I must confess you are in the hardest luck of any person I ever knew; but really, my dear sir, I don't see how I can render you any assistance, so we might as well consider the interview at an end. Now that I am better acquainted with you I will say, however, that if it gives you any pleasure to loll around here or to sleep up there in my cloisonné jar with the rose leaves, you are welcome to do so."

"If you would only hear my story, Hopkins," said the spirit, beseechingly, "you would be so wrought up by its horrible details that you would devise some plan for my relief. You would be less than a man if you did not, and I am told that you Americans are great fighters. Take this case for me, won't you?"

Hopkins hesitated. He was strongly inclined to yield, the cause was so extraordinary, and yet he could not in a moment overcome his strongly-cultivated repugnance to burdening himself with a client. Then he was conscientious, too. He did not wish to identify the famous house of Toppleton, Morley, Harkins, Perkins, Mawson, Bronson, Smithers and Hicks with a case in which the possibilities of success seemed so remote. On the other hand he could not but reflect that, aside from the purely humane aspect of the matter, a successful issue would redound to the everlasting glory of himself and his partners over the sea —that is, it would if anybody could be made to believe in the existence of such a case. He realized that the emergency was one which must be met by himself alone, because he was thoroughly convinced that the hard-headed practical men of affairs whom he represented would scarcely credit his account of the occurrences of the last hour, and would set him down either as having been under the influence of drink or as having lost his senses. He would not have believed the story himself if some one else had told it to him, and he could not expect his partners in New York to be any more credulous than he would have been.

His hesitation was short-lived, however, for in a moment it was dispelled by a sigh from his unseen guest. It was the most heartrending sigh he had ever heard, and it overcame his scruples.

"By George!" he said, "I will listen to your

story, and I'll help you if I can, only you will unstring my nerves unless you get yourself a shape of some kind or other. It makes my blood run cold to sit here and bandy words with an absolute nonentity."

"I don't know where I can get a shape," returned the spirit.

"What did the thief who took your shape do with his old one?" asked Hopkins.

"He'd buried it before I met him," returned the spirit.

"Buried it? Oh, Heavens!" cried Hopkins, seizing his hat. "Let's get out of this and take a little fresh air; if we don't, I'll go mad. Come," he added, addressing the spirit, "we'll run over to the Lowther Arcade and buy a form. If we can't find anything better we'll get a wooden Indian or a French doll, or anything having human semblance so that you can climb into it and lessen the infernal uncanniness of your disembodiment."

Hopkins rang the janitor's bell again, and when that worthy appeared he had him unfasten the door from the outside; then he and the spirit started out in search of an embodiment for the exiled soul.

"Hi thinks as 'ow 'e must be craizy," said the janitor, as Toppleton disappeared around the corner in animated conversation with his invisible client. "E's' talkin' away like hall possessed, hand nobody as hi can see within hearshot. These Hamericans is nothink much has far as 'ead goes."

As for Toppleton and the Presence, they found in the Lowther Arcade just what they wanted—an Aunt Sallie with a hollow head, into which the spirit was able to enter, and from which it told its tale of woe, sitting, bodily and visibly, in the rocking-chair, before the eyes of Hopkins Toppleton, the words falling fluently from the open lips of the dusky incubus the spirit had put on.

"It was odd, but not too infernally weird," said Hopkins afterwards, "and I was able to listen without losing my equanimity, to one of the meanest tales of robbery I ever heard."

CHAPTER V.

HOPKINS BECOMES BETTER ACQUAINTED WITH THE WEARY SPIRIT.

"I DO not know," said the weary spirit, as he entered the head of the Aunt Sallie and endeavoured to make himself comfortable therein, "I do not know whether I can do justice to my story in these limited head-quarters or not, but I can try. It isn't a good fit, this body isn't, and I cannot help being conscious that to your eyes I must appear as a blackamoor, which, to an English spirit of cultivation and refinement such as I am, is more or less discomfiting."

"I shouldn't mind if I were you," returned Hopkins. "It's very becoming to you; much more so, indeed, than that airy nothingness you had on when I first perceived you, and while your tale may be more or less affected by your consciousness of the strange, ready-made physiognomy you have assumed, I, nevertheless, can grasp it better than I might if you persisted in sounding off your woes from an empty rocking-chair, or from the edge of my cloisonné rose jar."

"Oh, I don't blame you, Toppleton," returned the spirit. "I am, on the contrary, very grateful to you for what you have done for me. I shall always appreciate your generosity, for instance, in buying me this shape in order to give me at least a semblance of individuality, and I assure you that if I can ever get back into my real body, I will work it to the verge of nervous prostration to serve you, should you stand in need of assistance in any way."

Hopkins' scrutiny of the Aunt Sallie, as these words issued from the round aperture in the red lips made originally to hold the pipe stem, but now used as a tubal exit for the tale of woe, was so searching that anything less stolid than the wooden head would have flinched. The Aunt Sallie stood it, however, without showing a trace of emotion, gazing steadfastly with her bright blue eyes out of the window, her eyelids more fixed than the stars themselves, since no sign of a wink or a twinkle did they give.

"I wish," said Toppleton, experiencing a slight return of his awed chilliness as he observed the unyielding fixity of Sallie's expression, "in fact, I earnestly wish we could have secured a ventriloquist's marionette instead of that thing you've got on. It would really be a blessing to me if you could wink your eyes, or wag your ears, or change your expression in some way or other."

"I don't see how it can be done," returned the spirit from behind Toppleton's back. "I cannot exercise any control over these wooden features."

Hopkins jumped two or three feet across the room, the unexpected locality of the voice gave him such a shock, and the pulsation of his heart leaped madly from the normal to the triply abnormal.

"Wh—whuh—what the devil did you do tha—that for?" he cried, as soon as he was calm enough to speak. "Do y—you want to give me heart failure?"

"Not I!" replied the spirit, once more returning to the Sallie. "That would be a very unbusiness-like proceeding on my part at a time like this, when, after thirty years of misery, I find at last one who is willing to champion my cause. I only wanted to see how my second self looked in this chair. To my eyes I appear rather plain and dusky-looking, but what's the odds? The figure will serve its purpose, and after all that's what we want.

I'm sorry to have frightened you, Toppleton, honestly sorry."

"Oh, never mind," rejoined Toppleton, graciously. "Only don't do it again. Let's have the tale now."

"Very well," said the spirit. "If you will kindly shove me further back into the chair, and arrange my overskirt for me, I'll begin— that's another uncomfortable thing about my situation at present. It's somewhat trying to a spirit of masculine habits to find himself arrayed in a shape wearing the habiliments of the other sex."

Hopkins did as he was requested, and, throwing himself down on his lounge, lit his pipe, and announced himself as ready to listen.

"I think I'd like a pipe myself," said the Sallie. "I've got a fine place for one, I see."

"How can you talk if you stop your mouth up with a pipe?" asked Hopkins.

"Through my nose," replied the spirit. "Or there are holes in the ears, I can talk through them quite as well."

"Well, I guess not," returned Hopkins. "I have had enough of your weird vocal exercises to-day without having you talk with your ears, but if you'll smoke with one or both of them, you're welcome to do it."

"Very well," replied the spirit. "I fancy

you're right, and inasmuch as I haven't had a pipe for thirty years, I'll let you fill up two for me, and I'll try 'em both."

Accordingly Hopkins filled two of the clay pipes, three dozen of which had come with the Aunt Sallie, and lighting them for the spirit, placed them in the ears of his vis-à-vis as requested.

"Ah," said the spirit as he began to puff, "this is what I call comfort." And then he began his story.

"I was born," he said, breathing forth a cloud of smoke from his right ear, "sixty years ago in a small house within a stone's throw of what is now the band stand in the park at Buxton."

"You must have had human catapults in those days," interrupted Toppleton, for as he remembered the band stand at Buxton, it was situated at some considerable distance from anything which in any degree represented a habitation in which one could begin life comfortably.

"I don't know about that. I am not telling you a sporting tale. I am simply narrating the events of my career, such as they are," returned the spirit, "and my father has assured me that the house in which I first saw light was, as I have said, within a stone's throw of what is now the band stand in the Buxton Park. The band stand may have been nearer the house in the old days than it is now,—that is an insignificant sort of a detail anyhow, and if you'd prefer it I will put it in this way: I was born at Buxton sixty years ago in a small house, no longer standing, from whose windows the band stand in the park might have been seen if there had been one there. How is that?"

"Perfectly satisfactory," replied Hopkins. "A statement of that kind would be accepted in any court in the land as veracious on the face of it, whereas we might be called upon to prove that other tale, which between you and me had about it a distinctly Munchausenesque flavour."

The spirit was evidently much impressed with this reasoning, for he forgot himself for a moment, and inhaled some of the smoke, so that it came out between his lips instead of from his ears as before.

"I am glad to see you take such interest in the matter," he said after a moment's reflection. "We must indeed have an absolutely irrefragible story if we are to take it to court. I had not thought of that. But to resume. My parents were like most others of their class, poor but honest. My mother was a poetess with an annuity. My father was a non-resistant, a sort of forerunner of Tolstoï, with none of the latter's energy. He was content to live along oh my mother's annuity, leaving her for her own needs an undivided interest in the earnings of her pen."

"He was a gentleman of leisure, then," returned Hopkins, "with pronounced leanings towards the sedentary school of philosophy."

"That's it," replied the spirit. "That was my father in a nut-shell. He took things as they came—indeed that was his chief fault. As mother used to say, he not only took things as they came, but took all there was to take, so that there was never anything left for the rest of us. His non-resistant tendencies were almost a curse to the family. Why, he'd even listen to mother's poetry and not complain. If there were weeds in the garden, he would submit tamely, rather than take a hoe and eradicate them. He used to sigh once in awhile and condemn my mother's parents for leaving her so little that she could not afford to hire a man to keep our place in order, but further than this he did not murmur. My mother, on the other hand, was energetic in her special line. I've known that woman to turn out fifteen poems in a morning, and, at one time, I think it was the day of Victoria's coronation, she wrote an elegy on William the Fourth of sixty-eight stanzas, and a coronation ode that reached from one end of the parlour to the other,—doing it all between luncheon and dinner. Dinner was four hours late to be sure, but even that does not affect the wonderful quality of the achievement."

"Didn't your father resist that?" queried Toppleton, sympathetically.

"No," replied the spirit, "never uttered a complaint."

"He must have been an extraordinary man," observed Toppleton, shaking his head in wonder.

"He was," assented the spirit. "Father was a genius in his way; but he was born tired, and he never seemed able to outgrow it."

Here the spirit requested Toppleton's permission to leave the Aunt Sallie for a moment. The head was getting too full of smoke for comfort.

"I'll just sit over here on the waste basket until the smoke has a chance to get out," he said. "If I don't, it will be the ruin of me."

"All right," returned Toppleton. "I suppose when a man is reduced to nothing but a voice, it is rather destructive to his health to get diluted with tobacco smoke. But, I say, that was a pretty tough condition of affairs in your house I should say. Poetic mother, do-nothing father, small income and a baby. How did you manage to live?"

"Oh, we lived well enough," replied the spirit. "The income was large enough to pay the rent and keep father from hunger and thirst —particularly the latter. Mother, being a poet, didn't eat anything to speak of, and I fed on cow's milk. We had a cow chiefly because her appetite kept the grass cut, and when I came along she served an additional useful purpose. In the matter of clothing we did first rate. Mother's trousseau lasted as long as she did, and father never needed anything more than the suit he was married in. Inheriting my mother's poetic traits, and my father's tendency to let things come as they might and go as they would, it is hardly strange that as I grew older I became addicted to habits of indecision; that I lacked courage when a slight display of that quality meant success; that I was invariably found wanting in the little crises which make up existence in this sphere; that I always let slip the opportunities which were mine, and that at those tides of my own affairs which taken at the flood would have led on to fortune, I was always high and dry somewhere out of reach, and that, in consequence, all the voyage of my life has been bound in shallows and in miseries, as my mother would have said."

"Your mother must have been a diligent student of Shakespeare," Toppleton retorted, resenting the spirit's appropriation to his mother of the great singer's words, and also taking offence at the implied reflection upon his own reading.

"Yes, she was," replied the spirit unabashed. "In fact, my mother was so saturated—she was more than imbued—with the spirit of Shakespeare, that she was frequently unable to distinguish her own poems from his, a condition of affairs which was the cause, at one time, of her being charged with plagiarism, when she was in reality guilty of nothing worse than unconscious cerebration."

"That is an unfortunate disease when it develops into verbatim appropriation," said Toppleton, drily.

"Precisely my father's words," returned the spirit. "But the effect of such parental causes, as I have already said," continued the exiled soul, "was a pusillanimous offspring, which for the offspring in question, myself, was extremely disastrous. The poet in me was just sufficiently well developed to give me a malarious idea of life. In spite of my sex I was a poetess rather than a poet. I could begin an epic or a triolet without any trouble; but I never knew when to stop, a failing not necessarily fatal to an epic, but death to a triolet. The true climaxes of my lucubrations were generally avoided, and miserably inadequate compromises adopted in their stead. My muse was a snivelling, weak-kneed sort of creature, who, had she been of this earth, would have belonged to the ranks of those who are addicted to smelling-salts, influenza and imaginary troubles, and not the strong, picturesque, helpful female, calculated to goad a man on to immortality. I generally knew what was the right thing to do, but never had the courage to do it. That was my peculiarity, and it has brought me to this—to the level of a soul with no habitation save the effigy of a negress, provided for me by a charitably disposed chance acquaintance."

"You do not appear to have had a single redeeming feature," said Toppleton, some disgust manifested on his countenance, for to tell the truth he was thoroughly disappointed to learn that the spirit's moral cowardice had brought his trouble upon him.

"Oh, yes, I had," replied the spirit hastily, as if anxious to rehabilitate himself in his host's eyes. "I was strong in one particular. In matters pertaining to religion I was unusually strong. My very meekness rendered me so."

"Your kind of meekness isn't the kind that

F

inherits the earth, though," retorted Toppleton. "Meekness that means the abandonment of right for the sake of peace is a crime. Meekness that subverts self-respect is an offence against society. Meekness which is synonymous with pusillanimity is not the meekness which develops into true religious feeling."

"No; that is very true," said the spirit. "I do not deny one word of what you say; but I, nevertheless, was an extremely religious boy, nor did I change when I entered upon man's estate; and it is that strong religious fervour with which my spirit is still imbued that has made my cup so much the more bitter, since, as I have hinted, he who robbed me of my body has written pamphlets of the most shocking sort over my name, denouncing the Church and attempting to upset the whole fabric of Christianity."

"I am anxious to get to the details of the robbery," said Toppleton, with a smile of sympathy; "pass over your extreme youth and come to that."

"I will do so," replied the spirit, returning to the figure Toppleton had provided for him, the smoke having by this time evacuated his new habitation. "I will omit the details of my life up to the time when I became a lawyer and—"

HOPKINS BECOMES BETTER ACQUAINTED. 67

"You don't mean to say you *ever* became a lawyer?" interrupted Hopkins, incredulously.

"Why, certainly," replied the spirit; "I became a lawyer, and at the time I lost my body I was getting to be considered a famous one."

"How on earth, with your meekness, did you ever have the courage to take up a profession that requires nerve and an aggressive nature if success is to be sought after?" asked the American.

"It was that same fatal inability to make up my mind to do what my conscience prompted. It was another one of my compromises," returned the spirit, sadly. "I couldn't make up my mind between the pulpit and literature, so I compromised on the law, mastered it to a sufficient extent to be admitted to practice, and opened an office—the same room, by the way, as that in which you and I are seated at this moment."

"Do you remember any of your law now?" Toppleton asked uneasily, for he was afraid the spirit might discover how ignorant he was on the subject.

"Not a line of it," returned the spirit. "It has gone from me as completely as my name, my body, my auburn hair and my teeth. But I *was* a lawyer, and by slow degrees I built up a fair practice. People seemed to recognize how strong I was in matters of compromise, and cases that were not considered strong enough to take into court were brought to me in order that I might suggest methods of adjustment satisfactory to both parties. For three years I did a thriving business here, and for one whose knowledge of the law was limited I got along very well. I was one of the few barristers in London who had become well-known to litigants without ever having appeared in court, and I was very well satisfied with my prospects.

"Everything went smoothly with me until a few weeks after I had passed my thirtieth birthday, when a man came into my office and retained me in an inheritance case, in which the amount involved was thirty thousand pounds. He had been made defendant in a suit brought against him by his own brother for the recovery of that sum. It was a very complicated case, but the brother really had no valid claim to the money. The father of the two men, ten minutes before his death, had told my client in confidence that it was his desire that he should inherit sixty thousand pounds more than the other brother, telling him, however, that he must get it for himself, since the written will of the dying man provided that the two sons should share and share alike. In spasmodic gasps the old man added that he would find the money concealed in a secret drawer in an old desk up in the attic, in sixty one-thousand pound notes. My client, realizing that his father could not last many minutes longer, and feeling that his dying wishes should not be thwarted, rushed from the room to the attic, and after rummaging about for nine minutes, found the drawer and touched the secret spring. Unfortunately the day was a very damp one, and the drawer stuck, so that it was fully eleven minutes before the money was really in my client's hands. He shoved it into his pocket and went downstairs again, where he learned that his father had expired one minute before, or just ten minutes after he had left him.

"The other son not long after discovered what had been done, and after listening to my client's story, decided to contest his title to his share of the sixty thousand pounds, alleging that the money not having passed into my client's hands until after the testator's death, belonged to the estate, and could only be diverted therefrom upon the production of an instrument in writing over the deceased man's signature, duly witnessed. You see," added the spirit, "that was a very fine point."

"Yes, indeed!" said Toppleton; "it's the

kind of a point that I hope and pray may never puncture my professional epidermis, for I'll be hanged if I'd know what to advise. What did you do?"

"Ah!" sighed the spirit, "there's where the trouble came in. I studied that case diligently. I consulted every law book I could find. Every leading case on inheritance matters I read, marked, learned and inwardly digested, and I made up my mind that if we could prove that my client's watch was fast upon that occasion, and that the money was in his hands one minute before his father's death instead of one minute after it, the plaintiff would not have a leg to stand on. Then it occurred to me 'this means trouble.' It means a long and tedious litigation. It means defeat, appeal, victory, appeal, defeat, appeal, on, on through all the courts in Great Britain, and finally the House of Lords, the result being the loss to my client of every penny of the amount involved, even though he should ultimately win the suit, and the loss to me of sleep, the development of nerves and a career of unrelieved anxiety. Compromise was the proper course to be recommended."

"A proper conclusion, I should say," said Toppleton.

"I think so, too," replied the spirit, "and if I had only remained true to my instincts my client would have compromised, and I should have been spared all that followed. It would have been better for all concerned, for I should have been in possession of myself to-day, and my client by compromising would in the end have lost no more than he had to pay me for my services—fifteen thousand pounds."

" Phe—e—ew ! " whistled Hopkins. " That was a swindle ! "

" Yes, but I wasn't party to it, as you will shortly see. When I made up my mind that compromise was the best settlement of the case, all things considered, I sat down right here by this window to write to Mr. Baskins to that effect. It was a beastly night out. The wind shrieked through the court there, and it was cold enough to freeze the marrow in a grilled bone. I was just about to sign my communication to Mr. Baskins, when I heard a knock at the door.

" ' Come in,' I said.

" And then, Mr. Toppleton, as sure as I am sitting here in this Aunt Sallie talking to you, the door opened and then slowly closed, a light step was perceptible to the ear, moving across the carpet, and in a moment a rocking-chair owned by me began to sway to and fro, just as this one sways when I or you are sitting in it, but to my eyes there was absolutely nothing visible that had not always been in the room."

Hopkins began to feel chilly again.

"You mean to say that to all intents and purposes, an invisible being like yourself called on you as you have called on me?" he said in a minute, his breath coming in short, quick gasps.

"Precisely," returned the incumbent of the Aunt Sallie. "I was visited, even as you have been visited, by an invisible being, only my visitor did not remain invisible, for as I sprang to my feet, my whole being palpitant with terror, the lamp on my table sputtered and went out; and then I saw, sitting luminous in the dark, gazing at me with large, gaping, unfathomably deep green eyes, a creature having the semblance of a man, but of a man no longer of this earth."

CHAPTER VI.

THE SPIRIT UNFOLDS A HORRID TALE.

"IF ever a man had a right to swoon away, Hopkins," continued the spirit, his voice dropping to a whisper, "I was that man, and I presume I should have done so but for the everlasting spirit of compromise in my breast. The proper thing to do under the circumstances was manifestly to flop down on the carpet insensate, just as you did when I announced myself to you; and I assure you I had greater reason for so doing than you had, for my visitor had absolutely no limitations whatsoever in the line of the horrible. He was an affront to every sense, and not, like myself, trying only to the ear. To the sense of sight was he most horrible, and I would have given anything I possessed to be able to remove my eyes from his dreadful personality, with the long bony claws where you and I have fingers; with tight-drawn cheeks so transparent that through them could be seen his hideous jaws; with eyes which stared even when the lids closed over them; and, worst of all, his throbbing brain was visible as it worked inside his skull; and so bloodless of aspect was he withal, that the mind instinctively likened him to a fasting vampire."

"Excuse me!" groaned Hopkins, throwing himself down on the couch and burying his face in the pillow. "This is awful. I've crossed the ocean eight times, Sallie, and until now I have never known sea-sickness, but this—this vampire of yours is mightier than Neptune; just hand me the whiskey."

"I'm sorry it affects you that way, Hopkins," said the spirit, "and I'd gladly give you the whiskey if I could, but you know how circumscribed my abilities are. I haven't any hand to hand it with."

"Never mind," said Hopkins, the colour returning to his cheeks, "I feel better now. It was only a sudden turn I had; only, my friend, go slow on the horrible, will you?"

"I wish I could," replied the spirit sadly, "but the cause of truth requires that I tell you precisely what happened, omitting no single detail of the sickening totality. Perhaps, before I proceed, you had better take a dozen grains of quinine, and have the whiskey within reach."

"That is a good suggestion," said Hopkins, rising and gulping down the pills, and grasping the neck of the square-cut bottle containing the treasured fluid, with his trembling hand. "Go ahead," he said, as he resumed his recumbent position on the couch.

"To the olfactories," resumed the spirit, "the visitant was stifling. A gross of sulphur matches let off all at once would be a weak imitation of the atmospheric condition of this room after he had been here two minutes, and yet I did not dare to turn from him to open the window. My only weapon of defence was my eye, under the tense gaze of which he seemed uneasy, and I was fearful of what might happen were I to permit it to waver for one instant. His colour was simply deadly. I should describe it best, perhaps, as of a pallid green in which there was a suggestion of yellow that heightened the general effect to the point where it became ghastly."

Here Hopkins' eyelids fluttered, and the bottle was raised to his lips. When the draught had been taken the bottle dropped from his nerveless fingers to the floor, and shivered into countless slivers of brown crystal.

"Jove!" ejaculated the spirit. "That was very unfortunate, Hop—"

"No matter," interrupted Hopkins, "it was empty. Go on. Did this private view you and the Nile-green apparition were having of each other last for ever?"

"No," returned the spirit, "it did not. It probably lasted less than a minute, although it seemed a century. I tried half a dozen times to speak, but my words were frozen on my lips."

"Why didn't you break them off and throw them at him?" suggested Toppleton, hysterical to the point of flippancy.

"Because I did not possess the genius of the Yankee who is inventive where the Briton is only enduring," retorted the spirit, somewhat disgusted at Toppleton's airy treatment of his awful situation. "Finally my visitor spoke, and for an instant I wished he hadn't, his voice was so abominably harsh, so jangling to every nerve in my body, however callous."

"'You don't appear to be glad to see me,' he said.

"'Well, to tell you the truth,' I replied, 'I am not. I am not a collector of optical delusions, nor am I a lover of the horrible and mysterious.'

"'But I am your friend,' remonstrated my visitor.

"'I should dislike to be judged by my friends, if that is so,' I returned, throwing as much withering contempt into my glance as I possibly could. 'I think,' I resumed, 'if I were to be seen walking down Piccadilly with you, I should be cut by every self-respecting acquaintance I have.'

"'You are an ungrateful wretch,' said the intruder. 'Here I have travelled myriads of miles to help you, and the minute I put in an appearance you cast worse slurs upon me than you would if I were your worst enemy.'

"'I do not wish to be ungrateful,' I answered coolly, 'but you must admit that it is difficult for a purely mortal being like myself to receive a supernatural being like yourself with any degree of cordiality.'

"'Granted,' returned the spectre with a grin, which was more terrifying to me than anything I had yet seen, 'but when I tell you that I have come to befriend you—'

"'I don't call it friendly to scare a man to death; I don't call it friendly to steal invisibly into a man's office and choke him nearly to suffocation. It seems to me you might use some other style of cologne to advantage when you go calling on your friends, and if I had cheeks through which my whole molar system was visible to the outside world, I'd grow whiskers.'"

"My admiration for you has increased eighty-seven per cent.," put in Toppleton, "that is, it has if all you say you said to the spook is true."

"I'd swear to it," returned the spirit, the tone of his voice showing the gratification he felt at Toppleton's words. "I talked up to him all the time, though I was quaking inwardly from the start. He noticed it too, for he said practically what you have just remarked.

"'You command my highest admiration,' were his words. 'If you were as spunky as this all the time, you would not need my assistance, but you are not, and so I have come. *You must not compromise that case.*'

"Here the deadly green thing rose from the chair and approached me," continued the spirit, "and as he approached my terror increased, so it is no wonder that, when he got so near that I could feel his wretched soul-chilling breath upon my cheek, his luminous body towering above me as a giant towers over a dwarf, and repeated the words, '*you must not compromise that case,*' I should shrink back into a heap at the side of my desk, and reply, 'Certainly *not.*'"

THE SPIRIT UNFOLDS A HORRID TALE. 79

"'You have a splendid fighting chance,' he added, 'but it will be a bitter fight,—a fight, the winning of which will make you famous, but which you, by yourself, with all the law in Christendom on your side, could no more win than you could batter down the Tower of London with balls of putty.'

"'Then,' said I, 'I *must* compromise.'

"'No,' returned my visitor, 'for I am here to win the case for you.'

"'You will never be retained,' I retorted. 'You are a degree too foggy to be acceptable either to my client or to myself.'

"'I do not ask to be retained; but you must provide me with the means to appear in court. *You must leave your body and let me put it on.*'"

"That must have been a staggerer," said Hopkins. "Were you fool enough to give it to him without getting a receipt?"

"I was not fool enough to yield without persuasion," rejoined the spirit sadly, "but when he brought all the infernal power at his command into play to lure me on, I weakened, and when I weaken I am done for. Toppleton, that messenger of Satan promised me everything that was dear to my soul. The temptation of Faust was nowhere alongside of that which was placed before me as mine if I but chose to take it, and no price was asked save that one little privilege of being permitted to do the things which should make me rich, powerful and happy in the guise which I was to put off that the apparition might put it on. From my boyhood days I had wished to be rich and powerful, and from the hour in which I reached man's estate had I been in love, but hopelessly, since she I loved was ambitious, and would not consent to be mine until I had made my mark.

"'Alone,' said my visitor, 'you will never make your name illustrious. With my help you may—and consider what it means. Refuse my offer, and you will lead the dull, monotonous life of him who knows no success, to whose ears the plaudits of the world shall never come; you will live alone and uncared for, for she whom you love cannot become the wife of a failure. Accept my offer, and in a month you are famous, in a year you are rich, in an instant you are happy, for the heart you yearn toward will beat responsive to your own.'

"'But your motive!' I cried. 'Why should you do all this for me who know you not, and without a price?'

"'My reason,' returned that perjured instrument of malign fate, 'is my weakness. I love the world. I love the sensation of living. I love to hear the praises of man ringing in my ears. I am a lover of earth and earthly ways, with no hope of tasting the joys of earth save in your acquiescence. I am the soul of one departed. I have put off against my will the mortal habitation in which I dwelt for many happy years. I have solved the rebus of existence and have put on omniscience. All things I can accomplish once I have the means. I ask you for them, with little hope that you will grant my request, however, because you are the embodiment of all that is uncertain. Had you lived among the Olympian gods, they would have made you the Deity of Indecision; but before refusing my offer remember this, you have now the grand opportunity of life, such an opportunity as has never been offered to any mortal being since the time of Shakespeare—'

"'Did Shakespeare have this opportunity?' I asked eagerly.

"'My son,' returned the apparition, with a meaning look, 'do not seek to know too much about the mystery of William Shakespeare. You know whence he sprang, how he lived and what he achieved; let my unguarded words of a moment since be the seed of suggestion which planted in the soil of your brain may sprout and blossom forth into the flowers of certain knowledge. It is not for me to let a mortal like you into the confidence of the Fates; suffice it that *I* offer you immortality and present happiness. Think it over: I will return to-morrow.'

"Before I could reply," continued the spirit, "he had vanished. The light of my lamp returned of its own volition, and but for the odour of sulphur which still clung to the hangings of the room I should have supposed that I had been dreaming.

"Utterly wearied by the excitement of my strange experience, I threw myself down upon my couch, and fell into a deep sleep from which I did not awake for sixteen hours, in consequence of which a whole day was practically gone out of my life.

"Darkness was closing in upon me as I opened my eyes, and as it grew more dense I could see taking shape in the chair by my table my visitor of the night before, more pallid and sulphurous than ever.

"'Well?' he said, as I opened my eyes.

"'No!' I answered shortly, 'I am not well. I might be much better if you'd confine yourself to the cemetery to which you belong.'

"'Reparteedious as ever!' he retorted.

"'I don't know the word,' I replied; 'it belongs to neither a dead nor a live language.'

"'But it's a good word, nevertheless,' observed the ghost quietly, 'and I advise you to think of it whenever you are inclined to indulge in stupid repartee. It may help you in your career,—but I have come for an answer to my proposition.'"

"He was right about reparteedious," said Hopkins, interrupting the spirit's story; "that's a good word, and unless you have it copyrighted I think I'll open the doors of my vocabulary and admit it to the charmed circle of my verbiage."

"No, I have no copyright on it," replied the spirit, gazing at Hopkins with as sad an expression as could possibly be assumed, considering the imperturbability of Aunt Sallie's countenance. "You may have it for your vocabulary, Hopkins, but if you will take a little well-meant advice you had better be very careful about your word collection. Your frequent and flippant interruptions of my sad story lead me to fear that you are overworking your vocabulary, which is a very dangerous thing for a young man of your age and intelligence to do.

"But to resume my tale," continued the spirit, after waiting a moment for Hopkins to reply to his suggestion, which Hopkins seemed not to hear, so busy was he looking for his memorandum book on his table,—a table so littered up with papers and silver paraphernalia for writing that no portion of its polished surface was visible. " I told my unwelcome guest that I had no answer to give him; that, as I was not a believer in the supernatural, I did not intend to waste my time in parleying with a figment of my brain.

"'You are cautious enough to have been a policeman,' he said in response to this. 'But caution in this instance is a vice.'

"'Caution is not a vice when a spirit of your evil aspect enters one's office in the dead of night, and asks for the loan of one's body,' I answered. 'I should be more justified in lending my diamond-stud to a sneak thief to wear to a lawn-tennis party at the Duke of Devonshire's, than in acquiescing in your scheme.'

"'Then you do not care to become a great man, to assure yourself of a fortune beyond your wildest dreams, to put yourself in such a position that she whom you love will be unable to resist your proposal of marriage?'

"'I am not untruthful enough to make any such pretence as that,' I answered. 'I do want to be everything you say, to have everything that you promise, but if I know the young woman upon whom my affections are lavishing themselves, she would object strenuously to my making a bargain with a transparent offshoot of the infernal regions like yourself. How do I know that, after I am married and have settled down to a life of honourable ease, you will not come along and insist upon an invitation to dinner; or obtrude yourself into the home circle at times when it will be extremely inconvenient to receive you? What guarantee have I that, when I have suddenly developed from my present obscurity into the promised distinction, you will not appear to some of my rivals and let them into the secret of my success; and, more important still, how do I know that after Miss Hicksworthy-Johnstone has become my wife you will not go to her and destroy my happiness by revealing to her the true state of affairs?'

"'I can only give you my word that I will be faithful,' returned my visitor.

"'Well, if your word is no better than reparteedious, it is not the kind of word upon which I should place any reliance whatsoever,' I retorted; 'so you may as well take yourself off; I am not lending myself these days.'"

"That was very well said," observed Toppleton, "only I wish you had had witnesses. Your sudden development of back-bone under the circumstance was so extraordinarily extraordinary that it is almost beyond credence. Did the fiend depart as you spoke those words?"

"No," returned the exiled spirit, "he did

not. He began operations, deceiving me grossly. He rose from the rocking-chair and said he fancied it was time for him to be off. When he got to the door he turned and kissed his right collection of claws to me, and asked if there was any place in the neighbourhood where he could get a drink. Well, of course, unpleasant as he was to look at, he had injured me in no respect, and save for my instinctive suspicions I had no real reason for believing that he was actuated by any but the best of motives. So I replied that the best place I knew of for him to get a drink was right here in this room, and that if he would wait a second I would join him in a glass. He hesitated an instant, and then said that seeing it was I who asked him, he thought he would; so I got out my little stone jug and poured out two rather stiff doses of brandy. Now it had been my habit to take my liquid refreshment undiluted, and taking my glass in hand I held it aloft and observed, 'Here's to you.'

"My visitor placed his claws on my arm.

"'You do not mean to say,' he said, 'that you take this fiery stuff without water?'

"'That is my custom,' I answered. 'I think it a positive wrong to spoil good brandy with the rather inferior brand of water we get here in

London, nor do I deem it proper to take so pure a fluid as water and destroy its innocence by introducing this liquid into it.'

"'As you please,' was my visitor's response. 'I was foolish enough to do that myself when I was fortunate enough to have a physique. In fact it was just that thing that finally laid me by the heels. But let me have a little water with mine please.'

"I laid my glass down beside his on the table, and, taking the pitcher, left the room for an instant to fill it at the water-cooler."

"That was a fine thing to do," said Toppleton. "Your idiocy cropped out then in great shape. How did you know he wouldn't rob you?"

"I wish he had robbed me and gone about his business," returned the spirit. "If that was all he did, I'd have been all right to this day. I was gone about two minutes, and when I returned he was standing by the window, whistling the most obnoxious tune I ever heard. What it was I don't know, but it gave me a chill. As I entered the room he stopped whistling and turned to greet me, took the pitcher from my hand, filled his glass to the brim with water and quaffed its contents. I drank my dose raw. As the brandy coursed down my throat into my stomach I fairly groaned with pain, it burned me so.

"'What the devil have you been doing with that brandy?' I cried, turning upon my visitor.

"'Swallowing it; why?' he asked innocently. 'You meant that I should drink it, didn't you?'

"'You can't put me off that way,' I groaned in my agony; for if I had swallowed a hot coal I could not have suffered more, that infernal stuff scorched me so. 'You have drugged my brandy.'

"'Have I?' he asked, with a menacing gesture and a frown that wrinkled up his hideous forehead, until his brains, still visible through the transparent flesh and bone, were reduced to a spongy mass no bigger than a walnut—"

"He was concentrating his mind, I suppose?" suggested Hopkins.

"It looked that way," said the spirit, "and it was an awful sight.

"'Have I?' he repeated, and then he added, 'well, if I have, it is only to save you from yourself, for by this means alone can you ever fulfil your destiny.'

"As these words issued forth from his white lips, I became unconscious. How long I remained so, I do not know; but when I came to once more, I was as I am now—a spirit having no visible shape; while seated in my chair, writing with my pen and in perfect imitation of my chirography, I saw what had been my body now occupied by another."

CHAPTER VII.

A CHAPTER OF PROFIT AND LOSS.

So overcome was the occupant of the Aunt Sallie at this point of his story, that he requested Hopkins' permission to leave his quarters that he might sit on the floor near the slivers of the shattered whiskey bottle. He needed stimulant. Hopkins readily granted the request, for he felt as if he would not mind having a little stimulant for himself, but as the last drop available for his purposes had been put to the use for which it was intended, he had to deny himself the comfort he would have derived from it. The fact that this horrid event, the harrowing details of which he had just listened to, had occurred right there in his own apartments served to make him doubly depressed, for it certainly indicated that the room, despite its cheerful situation, had been the dwelling-place of a supernatural being, and the present lessee was fearful lest that being should appear on the

A CHAPTER OF PROFIT AND LOSS. 91

scene once more to practise some of his infernal tricks upon him.

"You mean to say that when you recovered your senses, you had been deprived of your body?" said Hopkins at last, breaking the silence more for the sake of calming his agitated mind than because he had anything to say.

"Yes," replied the spirit. "I lay there on the sofa an intellectual abstract whose concrete had been amputated and invested by a being who had already lived four-score of years in one body, and who, having worn that out, was now on the look-out for a second. The sensation was dreadful, and when I attempted to do what theretofore I had always done in moments of extreme agitation—to pull fiercely at my moustache—I was simply appalled to realize that the power to raise my hand to do this had passed, along with the moustache itself, into the control of that other being. Then an access of rage surged over me, and I attempted to stamp my foot and shriek. The shriek was a success, but my foot like my arm was beyond my control.

"As the shriek died away I observed my head slowly turning from the paper before it on the table, my right hand relaxed its grasp on the pen, and my own eyes were turned upon me, and I was simply maddened to see the left eye wink mischievously at me, while my mouth broadened into a smile at my own misfortunes.

"'Hello,' I said to myself—that is you know the other being in myself said this to me outside of myself. 'You've come to, at last, eh? I thought you were going to remain in a comatose state for ever.'

"'See here, my friend,' I said, trying to be calm. 'This is a very clever trick you've put upon me, but from my point of view it is most uncomfortable, and I'd just as lief have you evacuate the premises, and permit me once more to assume my normal condition.'

"'Not until I have accomplished what I set out to accomplish,' was the answer that fell from my own lips, which again indulged in an impertinent smile at my expense. 'You don't suppose that I have put in three weeks of time and energy to make you famous with the intention of withdrawing on the eve of success, do you?'

"'I don't know what you mean,' I replied, 'I don't understand the allusion, nor can I see why you permit me to be insulted by my own lips.'

"Here," said the spirit, "my face became clouded and my smile vanished.

"'Ungrateful wretch that you are!' said he who had rifled me of myself. 'Are you not aware that three weeks have elapsed since you and your body parted company? Are you not aware that in that time I have forced the fight between the brothers Baskins to a point that has made that case the talk of London, and you, the hero of the hour in legal circles? Do you not understand that to-morrow you are to appear in court to sum up for your side, and that the London *Times* itself is to have five stenographers in court to take down every word that is uttered by him they call a second Burke, because of his eloquence, by him they call a second Sheridan, because of his wit, by him they call the newly discovered leader of the English bar, because of the aggressive and powerful manner in which this now celebrated will case has been conducted? And finally, are you not aware that it is you who gain the credit due to me, since it is I who have merged my personality into yours, while you have only to remain quiescent and accord to me the undisturbed occupation of your physical self for a few days more?'

"I know none of these things,' I answered. 'I know that possibly an hour ago you robbed me of my senses by your infernal machinations, and that when they are restored to me I find myself disembodied, nameless, invisible."

"'Do you know the date upon which I visited you first?' asked my tormentor.

"'Yes, it was November eighth. You returned on the night of November ninth—that is you returned early this evening.'

"'Perhaps this will convince you of the lapse of time, then,' retorted the occupant of my chair, tossing me a copy of the *Times*, 'and these will prove the rest,' he added, throwing several other newspapers at the place where my feet would have been had he not deprived me of them.

"I looked the papers over. The *Times* was dated November twenty-ninth and contained, as did also the others, a long account of the trial of the case of Baskins *v.* Baskins, in which I seemed to have figured prominently, concluding with a biographical sketch of myself coupled with the announcement that my former neighbours at Buxton were thinking of calling upon me to stand for Parliament. The tenour of everything in the papers was complimentary in the highest degree. It seemed that I had fairly routed my client's adversaries by nothing else than the aggressive manner of my fighting; that the case was practically won, though it still remained for me to sum up on the morrow, and that all London was expected to swarm into the court room to listen to my marvellous

A CHAPTER OF PROFIT AND LOSS. 95

eloquence. I read and was stunned. My position was more unhappy than ever, for here was a greatness builded up for me, that was utterly beyond my ability once returned to my corse of clay to sustain, and before me was placed the horrible alternative of perpetual exile or stultification."

" Lovely prospect," murmured Hopkins.

"As I read on," continued the spirit, " I felt the burning gaze of my visitor upon me, though he could not see me. In my body or out of it, he still possessed that fearful power of mental concentration which when exerted upon another through the medium of the eye was withering to the soul. So nervous did I become, that noiseless as a sun-mote I moved across to the other side of the room, and yet his gaze followed me as if instinctively aware of my slightest move. For a time not a word was spoken by either of us. I was so overcome at the sudden revelation of my fame, that I knew not what to say. The words of blame that entered into my consciousness—for that was all that was left of me—to say, I could not utter, because however badly I had been treated by this fearful creature in the beginning, it could not be denied that he had exerted his powers entirely for my benefit. On the other hand, I found it impossible to thank him for what he had done, since I was unable to dismiss the sense of indignation I felt at the summary and tricky manner in which he had robbed me of my individuality. As for the other, he seemed to be thinking deeply, which contributed to my alarm, for I knew not what it was he was revolving in his mind, and I feared some additional exercise of his supernatural power to my further discomfiture. Finally he spoke.

"'I am very deeply disappointed in you,' he said. 'I at least supposed you to be a person of gratitude. I deemed your nature to be sufficiently refined and sensible to favours to evince some little appreciation of what has been done for you, but I must say that the veriest clod of a peasant would be hardly less stolid n the face of generous effort in his behalf than you have been toward me. A more unresponsive soul than yours can hardly have lived.'

"'Can you blame me for not being effusively grateful to you for having cut me out of three weeks of existence?' I asked.

"'I can and I do,' he replied. 'You have not been incommoded. Upon your own confession you have not even been conscious during the period that you lacked anatomy. On the other hand, consider what I have gone through! I have suffered more in the past fortnight than I did in my whole previous life. In making the substitution of my inner self for yours in your body, I failed to remember how much greater than the mortal mind is the mind which has put on omniscience, and I have found the head in which your intellect lived at ease, so contracted, so narrow for the accommodation of mine, that the work I have undertaken in your interest has been one prolonged bit of unremitting agony. If you have ever tried to wear a shoe fifteen sizes too small for you, you will have a faint glimmering of the pain I have suffered in trying to encase a number thirty mind in a seven and a quarter head. It has been almost impossible for me to get some of my great thoughts into this thick cranium of yours in their entirety,—indeed if thoughts were visible, your client might have seen them sticking out of these ears, or hovering above this lovely halo of auburn hair you wear, waiting for admission to an already overcrowded skull.'

"As he spoke these words," said the spirit, with a chuckle, "I would have given ten pounds to have had something to smile with. I never thought one could miss his lips so much as when I tried to grin and found I had not the wherewithal. Despite the insulting comment of my visitor upon the quality of my own mind, it really filled what there was left of me with pleasure to hear that, even though I had departed from it, my body through its limitations had been able to resent the intrusion of this alien spirit so effectually.

"'In addition to the bad fit mentally,' continued the usurper of my anatomy, ' I have had to cope with your dyspepsia, which I did not know you had, and various other physical troubles such as rheumatism and toothache. It appears to me that even if I had not made you famous, the mere fact that I have relieved you of your toothache and rheumatism for three weeks should entitle me to your gratitude. However, I am willing to withdraw in your favour immediately if you insist. Of course you will have to sum up that case to-morrow, and I sincerely hope that you will do it in a manner creditable to your new self, that is to yourself as I have made you.'

" Of course you see, Hopkins," said the spirit, pausing in his story for a moment, "what a dreadful position that left me in. I was absolutely in the dark as to what had been done in the case. I did not know what line of argument had been pursued—I was even unacquainted with the name of the presiding justice at the trial, and as for the testimony elicited during the three weeks of my own personal desuetude, I had not read one word of it. To attempt to sum up the case under the circumstances meant ruin—it meant the final sacrifice of all my hopes; disgrace was imminent.

"'I cannot sum up the case,' I answered in a moment. 'I have not mastered the details, nor is there time for me to do so before the court opens.'

"'I am aware of that fact,' retorted the other. 'But that is nothing to me. I am not at all interested in upholding the undeserved fame of an ingrate. It's nothing to me if disgrace stares you in the face. My name is safe; graven upon a white marble stone in a country cemetery, it is beyond the reach of dishonour, and is endorsed in deep-cut letters with an epitaph extolling the virtues of him who bore it. This is your affair entirely; I wash my hands of it. Come, prepare for your return.'

"Now I submit to you, Hopkins, that, considering the situation, I was justified in changing my tone toward him. Put yourself in my place for a moment," said the spirit.

"I'd rather not," returned Hopkins with a shudder.

"Oh, I don't mean for you to exchange places with me. I just want you to try to imagine what you would have done under the circumstances. You would have besought him even as I did to crown his work with final success, and not leave matters in so unsatisfactory a condition; to spare you the dishonour of a public failure, wouldn't you?"

"Yes, either that or suicide would have been my course," returned Hopkins. "I think I'd have fled to some apothecary's and concealed myself in a chloroform bottle until my consciousness evaporated if I'd been you. You must have known that this thing could not keep up for ever, unless you would consent to remain disembodied all your days."

"That was just the most horrible thing about it," said the spirit. "When I realized what it all meant, I was nearly distracted; but believing suicide to be a crime, and knowing, as I have already told you, that the mind is indestructible, I could not do as you suggested. I might have lulled myself into a state of perpetual unconsciousness, but I did not care to do that, for the reason that, despite the harrowing features of my situation, I was morbidly interested to see how it would all come out. At any rate, I succumbed to my fears, and begged him not to think of departing from my mortal habitation and leaving me in the lurch.

"'Now,' he replied, his face, or rather my

face, wreathing with smiles, ' now you are talking sense. I thought you would come to it. It would be the height of folly for you to ruin yourself simply to gratify your love of retaining your form. I promise you that to-morrow night, after the great speech has been made in court—a speech which will ring out through the whole country, that will echo from the hills of Scotland across the Atlantic Ocean to the Rocky Mountains, to re-echo thence to the Himalayas, and so on until your fame has encircled the earth—I promise you that then I will depart hence and trouble you no more, except it be your desire that I return.'"

" That was a fair proposition—he wasn't such a mean fiend after all," said Hopkins.

" At that moment I thought he was rather a square fiend," returned the spirit sadly ; " but he developed as time went on."

" And the speech next day ? How was that ? Did he keep his word ? " Hopkins asked.

" Indeed he did," said the spirit with enthusiasm, " and it was simply marvellous. That night, after we had had the conversation I have just told you of, that fellow worked like a slave getting up his points, consulting the records, classifying the testimony and making notes for his great oratorical effort. Hardly a poet in the history of literature was there who did not contribute some little line or two to make the speech more interesting, or to emphasize some point in a manner certain to appeal to a polished mind or overawe an uncultivated one. Greek and Latin authors were levied upon for tribute. Parallels in ancient and modern history utterly unknown to me were instituted for the elucidation of the arguments advanced—in short, a more polished bit of oratory than that prepared for my tongue to utter never fell from mortal lips before, and as for the peroration—well, it would require the consummate art of the fiend himself adequately to describe it. It was simply dazzling.

"'There is only one drawback, one thing I fear for to-morrow,' said the fiend, as he finished his preparations, 'and that is that these miserable mortal lungs of yours will not be able to do justice to that speech, and some of these quotations rasp on your unpractised tongue, so that I fear their effect may be weakened. However, I'll do the best I can with poor tools; but one thing is certain, you must make a sacrifice to me who have sacrificed time and comfort to you.'

"'What is that?' I asked.

"'I cannot properly accent my words with your teeth in their present condition. For instance these words here: *And, gentlemen of the jury, what have we to say of the plaintiff in this action, the brother of the defendant and the first-born son of the decedent whose desires he now seeks to have over-ridden by the laws of this land, what have we to say of him? What palliation can he offer for his unfraternal conduct in thus dragging his own brother into the courts of this land in a mad effort to recover the paltry sum of thirty thousand pounds? History affords no parallel, gentlemen of the jury, to this cause of son living arrayed against his parent gone before, of brother fighting brother for a miserable pittance,* and so on. Don't you see that to be spoken impressively these words demand a certain venomous hiss? I want to electrify the jury by that hiss, but I can't do it unless I have out two of your back teeth and this front one.'

"Here he tapped the left of my two front teeth—pearls they were, Hopkins, pearls beyond price. Of course I objected.

"'I can't let you do that,' I said, 'it'll ruin my personal appearance.'

"'Bah, man!' he said. 'What is personal appearance to pre-eminent success? What are looks compared to immortality? I must again take advantage of your helplessness and rescue you from the effects of your own indecision. I have arranged to have a dentist here to-morrow morning at eight. In five minutes he will have the teeth out, and by noon your seething voice will have turned twelve good men and true into a mass of goose flesh that will be utterly unable to resist you.'"

Hopkins was heartless enough to laugh at this unexpected development.

"I wish I could appreciate the joke, Hopkins," said the spirit indignantly. "What is fun for you was tragedy for me. I had always prided myself on the vigour of my voice. There was nothing weak or affected about it, nor would I, had I been in control of my being, have permitted such vandalism as was perpetrated by that dentist the next morning, just for the sake of making a *coup* with the jury. I can't deny, however, that when the speech was delivered the general effect was heightened by the sibilant tone in which the words were spoken. To me the dreadful spirit within my body was apparent from introduction to peroration. The deadly greenness of the fiend shone out through every vein in my body. My eyes, once a beautiful blue, became like the eyes of an adder, and my cheeks took on a pallor that was horrible to look upon, and yet which so fascinated all beholders that they could not take their eyes away from it. The jurors sat petrified, terror depicted on every line of their faces; the judge himself, a florid, phlegmatic person ordinarily, was pale as a sheet and uneasy as an exposed nerve, and when my poor innocent finger, once so prettily pink of hue, was pointed, absolutely livid with the scorn that that creature alone could throw into it, at the terror-stricken plaintiff, he actually fell backward into convulsions, and was carried shrieking profanely from the court-room.

"As for me, I sat cowering directly behind the jury-box fearful for the future, fearful for the effect upon my poor body of the terrible strain that was put upon it, and wondering what I could possibly do upon resuming my normal condition to maintain the reputation which that morning's achievement had brought to me. So absorbed was I in these reflections that the judge's faltering charge at the conclusion of the proceedings fell upon my consciousness unheard, save as the monotonous roar of the vehicles in the street outside was heard; but the verdict of the jury, rendered without leaving the box, in favour of my client did reach my ears, and almost simultaneously came the announcement that there would be no appeal, since the plaintiff in the cause had been frightened into imbecility by the fearful indictment of his character in the summing-up of the counsel for the defendant."

CHAPTER VIII.

FURTHER DEVELOPMENTS IN THE MAKING OF A NAME.

"You must have felt like a vest-pocket Byron, to wake up and find yourself famous that way," said Toppleton; "or, perhaps you found yourself *in*famous, eh? I don't know how it is here in England, but in America a lawyer who'd browbeat a poor innocent litigant into a state bordering upon lunacy, would be requested to move out of town."

"It all depends," returned the spirit. "If my substituted self had limited his brow-beating to the plaintiff, it might have made the reputation which I found awaiting me upon my return to my remains, one of infamy, but that was by no means the case. The judge himself succumbed to nervous prostration a week later, the jurors vanished like a pack of frightened hares immediately they were discharged, and even my client shook like a leaf when he felt my eyes resting upon him. As for my own proper self, I was the worst scared man of the lot; so, you see, it was a sort of universal awe that was inspired by the demeanour of my body that day, and one which commanded rather than invited respect."

"Did you find your head a little stretched when you got back into yourself again, or did he break his word and refuse to let you back?" queried Toppleton.

"Oh, he kept his word that time," replied the spirit. "After the trial was over he took a cab and drove rapidly out to Regent's Park and back, returning to my chambers about six o'clock. I was there waiting for him, ready to enter upon my usual anatomical ways once more. My client was also there, though, of course, unaware that I was present in spirit. I was very much amused to see how utterly unnerved poor Baskins was by the strange events of the day. Several times he muttered to himself remarks like, '*I didn't know he had it in him*,' and '*If I'd thought he was that kind of a man I'd have kept blessed clear of him. I wonder what he'll charge.*' And then every time there was a step or noise of any kind out in the corridor, he would straighten up nervously and stare at the door in a tense sort of fashion which showed that he dreaded meeting me. Once he put his hand in his pocket and pulled out a big duelling pistol which I was alarmed to note was loaded to the muzzle. It was evident that the awe which my new self had inspired in him amounted to positive fear.

"That duelling pistol put an end to my enjoyment of the situation," continued the spirit. "I was afraid he might be goaded into discharging a load of cold lead into my body. Of course, I didn't care to have that happen, and under the agitation of the moment I uttered an ejaculation of consternation. I never saw in all my experience a man so thoroughly frightened as Baskins was when the sound for which he could not account greeted his ear. He went on his knees and shook like a leaf, clasping his hands, as if in prayer, before his face, which turned a blue white. The pistol fell from his hands to the floor, and, as it did so, the door opened, and I saw myself standing on the sill, haggard of face, but not worn of spirit, for the supernatural brilliance of my eye as it caught sight of the pistol and realized at a flash just what the situation was, showed that the soul within was still unwearied by its effort.

"Then," added the spirit, his voice husky with the remembrance of his dishonour, "came an interview that makes me blush, even though I have no cheek on which to display that manifestation of shame. My body sprang forward as the pistol met my eye, and, snatching the weapon from the floor, flung it out through the window into the court, where it exploded, the jar of contact with the stone walk being sufficient to discharge it. As the sharp report of the pistol echoed through the court my client threw himself flat on his face, and prostrate there at my feet began to utter a string of incoherent lamentations and despairing requests for mercy at my hands which were painful to hear, and I judged from what meaning I could patch together from his jumble of words, that he deemed me an emissary of Satan,—and I think he was right.

"'What does this mean?' queried the fiend within me. 'Murder or suicide? If you contemplated suicide, I forgive you; if murder—'

"'I was afraid,' gasped my unhappy client. 'Your power was so terrible; the effect of your words so awful, that I—'

"'Ah!' interrupted the fiend. 'I see. It was murder you were prepared to do in case we should not agree, and the power of my eye should chance to be exerted to win you from your determination whatever it may have been.'

"'No—not that—not that!' shrieked my client. 'It was but the natural instinct of self-preservation that led me to—'

"'You weaken your cause by your loquacity, my friend,' said the fiend. 'You suspected me of contemplating some dishonourable or cowardly act, and for that reason you entered the office of him who has saved your good name and your purse alike from them who would have robbed you of both, having so little sense of gratitude that you bring with you an instrument of death. Very well, let it be so. I am satisfied if you are. I might do that to you now which would place you in far worse estate than your poor brother is in. If you had your pistol in your hand, aimed at my heart, you would still be powerless to do me an injury, for with one glance of my eye I could force you to turn the muzzle to your own head, and with another compel you to empty its leaden load into your own brains. Your suspicions are insulting, but an insult from one of your calibre to one of mine is as the sting of a fly to the elephant; I pass it over and charge it on the bill. Ten thousand pounds for trying the case, two thousand five hundred for accepting your insult, two thousand five hundred for condoning it, and in one hour must this money be in my hands with a letter—a letter written and signed by you, expressing your satisfaction with the manner of my conducting the case, and concluding with an allusion to your surprise that my charge is so moderate."

"'And if I refuse to submit to this outrage?' queried my client, lashed into a show of courage which he really did not feel.

"'You leave this room a raving maniac, for I have the power to make you so,' I was appalled to hear myself reply."

"And do you mean to tell me," said Hopkins, his bosom heaving with indignation, "that you sat there like a zero on a pedestal, and kept silent with this blackmailing infamy going on under your very eyes?"

"I was speechless with rage," returned the spirit, "or I should have interfered. Before I could recover my composure the letter had been written and the money paid, for my client still had the sixty thousand pounds in their original form, in the one thousand pound bank-notes. The struggle he went through was terrible to witness, and as the notes passed from his hands into mine he sighed like one who was heart-broken. The fiend dictated the letter commending my efforts, and expressing surprise that the amount asked for my services was so moderate, and then he opened the door and ushered the unfortunate victim out. As the latter left the room the fiend whispered to him in withering tones to beware of his vengeance if he ever attempted to reveal what had passed since he entered the room.

"'For,' said he, 'if you are not careful, it matters not in what part of this or any other world you may be, you must forever be within my reach, and forever subject to the consequences of my resentment.'

"Then," said the spirit, "he slammed the door violently and turned and fixed my eyes upon the corner wherein I sat aghast with the mortification of having my name identified in any man's mind with such a diabolical act as that I had just witnessed.

"Now,' he said, 'you may have this carcass of yours back and welcome. It's lucky for you I have the power I have. If I hadn't, your body would be riddled with bullets within twenty-four hours.'

"'Bah!' I replied. 'That man had no more intention of using that pistol without provocation than I have, and considering the terror with which you have managed to inspire every-one with whom you have come in contact to-day, I don't wonder he came armed.'

"'I never thought of that,' said my substitute, 'though what you say about everybody's terror is true; you might apply it even more broadly than you do, because as I drove down the Strand just now even the omnibus horses shied, and the driver of my cab had all he could do to keep his ramshackle steed from running away. But hurry up and get ready to relieve me of this mortal incubus of yours, and take your money—it's a nice little sum, eh?'

"'Magnificent,' I returned. 'And when you and I have changed places I am going to return all but five hundred pounds to that poor fellow you have just robbed in such a conscienceless fashion.'

"The moment I said this," said the spirit, "I regretted it, for he grasped the money with my right hand, and holding it over the fire, which was blazing merrily in the grate, he said. 'My friend, I exact from you an oath that you will not return one penny of this sum to Mr. Baskins. If you refuse, I shall cast every one of these bank notes into that fire, nor shall I admit you once more to your form until the very ashes of those notes have disappeared into the air.'

"Now what could I do under the circumstances, Toppleton?" asked the spirit earnestly. "Could I do anything but swear to what he asked?"

"Yes," returned Hopkins, "you could. I don't believe so vile a creature as he could have distinguished between a bible and a city directory. I'd have taken the oath on the city directory."

I

"Alas!" said the spirit sadly, and with such evident sincerity that it jostled the Aunt Sallie from the chair to the floor. "As I said to you before, I am only an enduring Briton where you have the inventive genius of the Yankee. I never thought of the substitution of the directory for the bible, and the consequent elimination of moral responsibility from the oath. I simply swore as he desired me to, and in an hour I was alone in my office, the occupant of a frame so exhausted that I could scarcely lift my head, and in my pockets were those miserable bank notes, more burning to my conscience than had they been sovereign for sovereign in gold coin hot from the mint."

"Of course," suggested Hopkins, "you devoted them to the cause of charity; subscribed all but your just due to the House for Imbeciles, in which that wronged unfortunate the plaintiff was incarcerated?"

"I intended something of the sort," returned the spirit, extricating himself from the head of Aunt Sallie, and ensconcing himself on the paper-weight on Hopkins' desk. "But I didn't have time. You see, immediately after the trial a perfect avalanche of litigants from other offices slid into mine, and within a week I was so overwhelmed with business that I had to hire the rest of this floor here to find room for my papers.

It was painful to me, too, to observe that those who had heard of my fame, but who had never seen me, were manifestly disappointed, when taking their departure at the close of a first interview, at having found me so much less great than they had been led to believe by the public estimate of my abilities. Nevertheless, cases of the most intricate sort were fairly dumped into my hands by the cart-load, and, worst of all, I found that eminence brought with it other responsibilities which I was ill-prepared to meet. I was constantly in receipt of requests to lecture on subjects of a variety that would have appalled the fiend himself, and worse than all I was called into consultation by the Crown in certain litigation of international importance. For a time I tried to go it alone, and by assiduous devotion to study to fit myself for the responsibilities which my fame had brought me, but it was impossible. I broke down in less than a month; but having tasted the joys of prominence I was not strong enough to resist the temptation to prolong it indefinitely, and, without thinking of the means, I committed myself to certain undertakings which were utterly beyond my intellectual strength to accomplish, and then, when brought face to face with failure and disgrace, there was but one thing left for me to do, and that I did.

"I summoned the fiend. The mere expression of a desire to see him was sufficient to bring him into my presence, and time and time again did I subject my poor body for ambition's sake to the dreadful interchange of spirits.

"From without I watched my development from mediocrity to fame with a joyous interest, not unmixed, however, with regret, for, at such moments as were permitted me to enjoy the undivided possession of myself, I could not but feel conscious of a diminution of physical strength which detracted materially from my happiness; and yet when day after day I saw my name in print, and noted that I was regarded as one of the most marvellous intellectual products of the day, I could not bring myself to the point where I could renounce everything I had gained, and withdraw to the contented life of the recluse. Let a man once taste a living immortality, Hopkins, and I care not how strong his character may be, he would part with all that he holds most dear sooner than he would renounce that.

"And so it went on for a full year. I became the leading light of the English bar; I astonished the world as a public orator; so potent were my arguments that in court or on the hustings none were able to resist me. At public dinners I was the speaker who alone could hold the feasters when the seductions of the wine cup awaited the cessation of my eloquence. Had I been able to extend the hours of my days from twenty-four to ten times twenty-four, I could not have responded to all the calls that were made upon my time. Then as if to show the world that one profession was too small to hold the boundless qualities of my genius, I startled the English reading public with a novel, the depth and power of which stirred the soul of the most *blasé* of novel-readers, and the presses of my publisher were taxed to the utmost to supply the demand for my work; then came a volume of poems which caused my name to be mentioned as a possible successor to the laureateship; then a series of essays on scientific and philosophical subjects which were nearly my undoing, since my omniscient self, as I came to call the fiend who was responsible for my greatness, was absent upon one occasion when I was called upon unexpectedly to receive a delegation of Scottish scientists, who had travelled from Edinburgh to London to consult with me in regard to certain propositions advanced in my book. What they thought of me Heaven only knows. You see, Hopkins, as far as my original self was concerned there wasn't an atom of scientific knowledge in my body, and to tell you the truth I hadn't even read my book, concerning which these unwelcome grey beards had come from Edinburgh to speak."

"I should like to have been on hand to hear you," said Hopkins with a laugh. "You must have felt like Damocles!"

"I was worse off than Damocles. He was face to face with nothing but death. I was having a *tête-à-tête* with dishonour. Damocles had a sword suspended over his head, held in place by a hair, I had a Krupp cannon over mine, held in place by Heaven knows what."

"How did you get out of it?" queried Hopkins. "Summon the fiend?"

"What, summon that deadly green thing before those men, and change places with him in the presence of witnesses? I fancy not. I have been a complete hall-marked fool in many respects, Hopkins, but my idiocy never went as far as that. The only thing left for me to do was to acquiesce in nine things that those fellows said, and look doubtful at the tenth and say I didn't know about that; my inherent love of compromise and my ingenuity in that direction stood me in good stead upon that occasion. It was a narrow squeak, but I got through all right. The *savants* went back to Edinburgh somewhat disappointed, I presume, with the new sun on the scientific horizon.

And you ought to have seen how the fiend laughed when I told him about it the next time I saw him! He fixed it all right, however, by sitting down and writing a letter to my late visitors and answering every one of their questions, and asking them a few additional ones, to answer which I fancy put them to their trumps.

"After making me famous as scientist, novelist and lawyer, the fiend induced a political bee to enter my cap, and one day after an absence of a week from my body, during which period of time I was utterly in the dark as to its whereabouts, I was appalled to see it reel in at the door in a maudlin state that revolted me.

"'Well,' I said as soon as I was able to speak, 'what new disgrace is this you have put upon me? Am I to make my mark now as an inebriate, or is this simply a little practical joke you are putting upon my sensibilities? If it is the latter, it is a mighty poor joke.'

"'No,' returned the fiend, who I am pleased to say showed some sense of shame at the plight he had got me into this time. 'No, this is not a practical joke, nor do I wish to ruin your reputation for sobriety. I regret this apparent liquidation of your system quite as much as you do, not because I care what others say, though. It is because I find it much harder to manage your body under these present circumstances. When one leg wants to go dancing down Pall Mall, and the other evinces a strange desire to walk gravely off in the direction of Scotland Yard, it is a most difficult thing for a mind not thoroughly in sympathy with either of them to drive them down the Strand in that modest, unassuming fashion which alone enables one to avoid police supervision. I've had the devil's own time with this weak corse of yours, and if I had known how abominably light-headed and airy-legged a little strong drink made you, I never should have had you stand for Parliament—'

"'Stand for Parliament?' I cried, aghast at the new honour which was being thrust upon me. 'Have I been standing for Parliament?'

"'Well, not exactly' laughed the fiend. 'You've been sort of held up for Parliament; you haven't been able to stand up without wobbling for five days; in fact, not since you tried to do your duty by your constituency, and take a little something at your own expense with a few rounds of doubtful voters. You were nearly defeated, my boy, because of your disgusting inability to cope with the flowing bowl, but I managed to pull you through. The temperance people voted to a man against you, but the other interests stood by you pretty well, and you now represent your old neighbours in—'

"'My old neighbours,' I moaned. 'Have I been made to appear to my old neighbours in the light of a dissipated politician when all my life long I had been known to them as a sober—'

"'Don't dwell on that point, my good fellow,' interrupted the fiend. 'Forget it. In forgetfulness of what you have been, and in consideration of what you have become, lies happiness. By the way—have you a mother living?'

"'Yes,' I answered, numb with anxiety for fear of what was coming. 'You haven't disgraced me in her eyes, have you?'

"'Oh, no,' returned the fiend. 'But a lady claiming to be your mother visited me during the campaign, and was very indignant because I failed to recognize her—that cost you some votes, but not enough to change the result. She didn't look a bit like you, and I was afraid the opposition was putting up some game on us, so I just laughed her off.'

"'You—you laughed her off—you mean to tell me,' I stammered, 'that when my mother came to my political headquarters to see her son, he refused to recognize her, and laughed her off?'

"'Oh, come,' said the fiend indignantly, 'don't get angry. Remember one thing, please. You are now a member of Parliament, a great Lawyer, a famous Scientist, a Novelist and an Orator. It is I who have made you so. If you don't like what I've done, we'll call the arrangement off, and you can make a spectacle of yourself in the eyes of the world. I hate an ingrate. You couldn't expect me to know a lady whom I never even saw before, and when I have a big scheme on foot I do not intend to have it spoiled for want of caution. If I made you seem an undutiful son, I am sorry for it, and will strive to make amends next time I meet your mother. I'll write a formal apology if you desire, but I don't wish to hear any more of your sentimental nonsense. Much has to be sacrificed in achieving greatness, and you have got there with just about as little personal inconvenience as any man in history. Stop your snivelling, or I'll desert your cause, and what that means even you can grasp.'

"With these words," concluded the spirit, " he departed, and left me to sleep off the effects of a seven days' campaign in which my moral welfare had been sacrificed to the thirst of at least four hundred doubtful voters. Credited with a seat in Parliament, I found my name debited with the crime of intemperance, lack of self-respect, and a gross affront to my own mother ; a fine record for one week in which in my own consciousness I was unable to recollect doing anything that could not have been done with propriety by a candidate for canonization."

"Humph!" ejaculated Toppleton, deeply moved by the horror of the weary spirit's story. "It strikes me that canonization in the form in which it was used on the Sepoys in '57 would be mild punishment for that Nile-green brute that got you into this. To tell you the truth, Sallie, the fearful justice of your cause is almost enough to make me withdraw entirely. I should hate to be called upon to prosecute a defendant of the nature of your verdant visitor."

CHAPTER IX.

THE CROWNING ACT OF INFAMY.

"Hear me to the end, Hopkins, I beseech you," said the exile earnestly. "Of course the fiend strikes you as a being to be avoided, but I do not believe that he is now as powerful and as terrible as he was in the days gone by. Long confinement to a purely mortal sphere must necessarily have weakened his supernatural powers, and it strikes me that properly managed by a young and aggressive lawyer, our case against him would be won in an instant. At all events, do not compel me to leave my story unfinished. I am sure that when you hear of the crowning act of infamy of which my evil genius was guilty, you will not hesitate a moment in making up your mind that duty summons you to aid me."

"Very well," rejoined Hopkins. "Go on with the tale, only do not be too sanguine as to its results in convincing me that I am the man to extricate you from this horrid plight."

"After I had attended one or two meetings of the House of Commons," said the exile, resuming the thread of his story, "I enjoyed the experience so much that I almost forgave the fiend for having so nearly ruined me with all my old friends; and having written, in accordance with his promise, a truly beautiful letter to my mother, explaining away the harsh treatment she had suffered at the hands of her now illustrious son on the ground of his not being quite himself on that occasion—a state of mind due to too close attention to work and study—I quite forgave him for that unpleasant episode in my campaign. My mother too overlooked the affront, and wrote me a most affectionate epistle, stating that I might trample upon her most cherished ideals with her entire acquiescence if my taking that course would ensure to her the receipt of so loving and touching a letter as the one I had sent her. The fiend and I both had to smile, on receiving my mother's note, to observe that the dear old lady attributed my ability to express myself in such beautiful terms to the poetic traits I had inherited from her.

"'She's very proud of her dear boy,' sneered the fiend.

"'In spite of his brutality at the committee-room,' I retorted; and then we both grinned.

for each truly believed that he had got the better of the other."

"It was a pretty close contest," said Hopkins. "But on the whole the laugh seems to be on you."

"It certainly was the first time I tried to speak in Parliament," returned the spirit. "Such a failure was never seen. I was to take part in a very important debate, and when the hour came for me to get on my feet and talk, I was my weak-kneed self and utterly unacquainted even with the side I was expected to take. The fiend had promised to do all the talking, and on this occasion failed to materialize. I spoke for ten minutes in an incoherent fashion, mouthing my words so that no one could understand a syllable that I uttered. It was a fearful disappointment to my friends in the House and in the galleries; the latter being packed when it was understood that I was to speak. Of course, when the fiend appeared later on, he straightened it all out, and the printed speech which he dictated and which I wrote was really a fine effort and did our party much good. But these little embarrassments were tragedies to me, and at every new success I quailed before the possibilities of disastrous failure at the next effort. In but one respect was I entirely free from the fiendish influence, and that was in the matter of my love. From that phase of my life the fiend kept himself apart, and it was the only joyous oasis to be found in the boundless desert of my misery. To the fiend, Sunday was literally a day of rest, for upon that day he never approached me, and I devoted it to calling upon the woman I loved.

"She was a beautiful woman, the only daughter of a retired city merchant, and fond of the admiration of successful men. That she loved me before I attained to eminence in the various professions in which the fiend had compelled me to dabble, I had much reason to believe; but I had never ventured to make love to her in dead earnest, because I feared for the result. She had often said to me that while she should never marry for riches and position, she did not intend to fall in love with any man just because he had neither, and that no man need ever propose marriage to her who was not reasonably sure of a successful career. It was not selfishness that led her to think and speak in this manner, but a realizing sense of the unhappy fact that mediocrity married is as hopeless as a broken-winded race-horse in harness. There is plenty of ambition but no future, and as she often said, 'Where hopelessness comes, happiness dwelleth not!'"

"A daughter of Solomon, I wot," interrupted Toppleton.

"Yes," said the spirit, with a sigh for her he had lost, "and rather superior to the old gentleman in a great many ways. Of course I understood, and, lacking achievement in my profession, discreetly held my tongue on the subject of matrimony, taking good care, however, when I called never to let any other fellow outstay me, unless perchance he was some poor drivelling idiot from whose immediate present the laurel was further removed than from my own. She understood me, I think, though I never put that point to a practical test by a proposal of marriage. This was the state of affairs at the time of my first meeting with the fiend, and for a year subsequent to that ill-starred night upon which he first crossed my path I let matters take their own course, waiting a favourable opportunity to ask the great question, upon the answer to which hung all my future happiness. I could see that with my increasing fame, her interest in me waxed; but as every passing day brought new and un-dreamed-of distinctions she grew more and more reserved toward me—a most feminine trait that, Hopkins. When a woman begins to love a man in dead earnest, in nine cases out of ten she will make him feel that he is utterly abhorrent to her, and it's a good thing she does, because it makes him look carefully into his own character in an endeavour to discover and to root out all the undesirable features thereof. It is this that enables love to redeem men whom the world considers irredeemable, so, of course, I had no feeling of discouragement at her growing coldness, for, understanding women, I knew exactly what it meant. I think I was more or less of an enigma to her."

"I should think it likely," said Toppleton. "If she really knew you, she must have been mightily surprised at your sudden strides towards universal genius. It's a wonder to me that she did not suspect the enigma, and give it up."

"Yes," returned the spirit. "It was very embarrassing to me when she expressed her surprise at my progress, and asked me how I did it, and other questions equally hard to answer. And then her father, who was always more or less insufferable, now became absolutely insulting—that is, his new found appreciation of my virtues led him into making assertions which galled me, he little knew how much—assertions to the effect that to look at me no one would suspect that I had more than ordinary intelligence; that to hear me talk one would never suppose I could make a speech of any kind,

K

much less set the world on fire by my eloquence; and finally, that no man after this could tell him that it was possible to judge of the future by the past, or the past by the present, for he had always thought me foredoomed to failure, and I had achieved success, and, having achieved success, gave no present evidence that I deserved it."

"He had the making of the accepted mother-in-law in him," said Hopkins. "What could have induced you to fall in love with the daughter of a man like that?"

"She was a superb woman, that's what," rejoined the spirit with enthusiasm, "and when I think of the happiness that the Nile-green shade first placed within my reach and then snatched from me, I regret that the soul is immortal, and that I am not all-powerful, for it would please me to grind his soul into absolute nothingness.

"It was at least a year and two months subsequent to my first meeting with him," continued the spirit as soon as his overwrought feelings would permit, "that he first broached the subject of matrimony. He had attended a grand ball at the house of the Earl of Piccadilly and was the lion of the occasion owing to his stand in certain recent Parliamentary crises. His readiness in debate had gained him a high

THE CROWNING ACT OF INFAMY. 131

position, and his natural grace of manner—that is, *my* natural grace of manner—had helped him to a hold on the affections of those with whom he was associated, for, as he grew more accustomed to my figure and got his angles comfortably rounded off to fit my curves, he managed to subdue that horrible aspect he had assumed with such fearful effect in the trial of Baskins *v.* Baskins, and when geniality was the attribute most likely to help him on he was geniality personified. The ball was ostensibly one of the Earl of Piccadilly's usual series of annual functions, but in reality it was given for the purpose of introducing me into society. From all accounts, it was a grand affair, and I seemed to have made as fine an impression as a social debutant as I had in the law courts, in the field of literature, and in the House of Commons. If the fiend spoke truly that night, when he returned and handed my fatigued body over to me for a rest, I made a marked success; all the ladies were raving about me; I was a divine dancer, though before that night my feet had never tripped to the strains of a waltz, polka, or any other terpsichorean exercise. I pleased the dowagers as well as the maids, and had, in short, become an eligible—that is I had become as desirable a matrimonial *parti* as an untitled person could hope to be, and the fiend remarked with a sly wink that it was not beyond the range of possibilities that the Premier would bestow upon me one of the peerages at his disposal when the proper time came.

"'Bachelorhood is pardonable in a young man,' said my evil genius upon this occasion, 'but we must marry if we are to reach the pinnacle of success. There is a solidity about the married man's estate that bachelorhood lacks, and I rather think I can make a match that will push us ahead.'

"'I don't think I need your assistance,' I replied. 'In fact I prefer that some of the things which pertain to myself shall be left entirely in my own hands. In matters of the affections I can take care of myself.'

"'Very well,' was the fiend's response. 'Have your own way about it, only take my advice and get married. We need a wife.'

"'We?' I cried. 'We! I just want you to understand, my dear sir, that the pronoun doesn't fit the case. *I* may need a wife and *you* may need a wife, but if you think I'm going into any co-operative scheme with you in that matter you are less omniscient than usual. Remember that please and let us have nothing more to say on the subject.'"

"That was a very proper stand for you to take," said Hopkins, gravely. "Though I think that, under the circumstances, you should have given up all ideas of marriage. No woman would have you, knowing that you were not yourself at times·; and then having as little control over your other self as you seem to have had, you would often have found yourself in hot water for flirting with other women, when, in reality, your own self was as innocent as a mountain daisy."

"I know I did wrong in thinking of marriage, Hopkins," returned the spirit, "but if you had ever met the woman I loved, you would have loved her too—yes, even if you were a confirmed celibate. I don't believe a Cardinal, sir, would have hesitated between his hat and her. My sole justification was her loveliness, and then the fiend's ready acquiescence in my statement that in that matter he must hold aloof gave me confidence that I might safely take the step I had so long and so ardently desired to take.

"Weeks passed by, and in everything save the courtship of Miss Hicksworthy-Johnstone I gave myself unreservedly over to the fiend, who began suddenly to take an interest in my personal appearance which he had never before manifested. He laid in a fine supply of clothes—dress suits, walking suits, lounging suits—suits in fact of every description and of the finest texture. Shirts and collars, and ties of the choicest sort were imported by him from Paris, and on my hands I now observed he was beginning to wear kid gloves of fashionable type. His hats and shoes were distinctly in the mode, and his jewelry, as far as it went, was of unexceptionable taste and quiet elegance. In fact, Toppleton, I began to be something of a dandy. This I attributed to the natural vanity of my other self. I, too, was proud of that graceful form, but I never thought enough about it to go about arraying it in a fashion which neither Solomon nor the lily of the field could ever have approached. I cared nothing for gloves save as a means to a warm finger's end, and it made no difference to me whether my hat was of the style of '48, or plucked fresh from the French Emperor's own block. As long as my head was covered I was satisfied. Patent leather shoes I could never bring myself to buy, because they had always seemed to me to go hand in hand either with poverty or laziness. To a man who cannot afford shoe blacking or who is too lazy to black his own boots, patent leathers, I thought, were a boon; but I never classed myself under either head, and wore the regular foot gear of the plain but honest son of toil.

"But now all was changed. My other self was vain, and unexpectedly gave himself over

THE CROWNING ACT OF INFAMY. 135

to dandyism. At first he rather disturbed my equanimity by wearing somewhat loud patterns, but he soon got over that, and between us, after a very little while, two or three months perhaps, my body had the best clothes there were to be had in all London. I had not realized all this time that I was fast becoming a millionaire, and when my tailor's bill for fifteen hundred pounds came home one night I was in a great stew, but the fiend came in and relieved my conscience very much by showing me my balance in the bank. It amounted, Toppleton, to one hundred and seventy-five thousand pounds, with an income still running evenly along from my law practice of ten thousand pounds per annum, not to mention the revenues from my books, which in six months had amounted to two thousand pounds. I was a rich man, and when I observed that this was my condition, I made up my mind to ask Miss Hicksworthy-Johnstone's hand in marriage the very next time I saw her. I hoped this would be soon, but, alas for human expectations, it was not. The Christmas holidays were about to begin, and I bethought me that at the season of goodwill toward men I might ask the possessor of my heart to accept it as a permanent gift, a decision which I unfortunately kept to myself, for from one end of the holidays to the other I never laid eyes upon my mortal habitation. The fiend was off with it for one whole month, Hopkins."

"Didn't you know where?" asked Toppleton.

"I did not," returned the spirit. "He went off with it as usual one night late in November to attend a meeting of the leaders of our party, telling me not to worry if he did not return for twenty-four hours, since there was important business on hand. What the business was he did not inform me, nor did I seek to know it, since under our arrangement it was not necessary that I should familiarize myself with parliamentary matters, which were usually as dry as they were weighty anyhow, and hence distasteful to me.

"Well, I waited twenty-four hours and no fiend appeared. Another day passed with no sign of him. A third day moved into the calendar of the past; a week elapsed, then a second, a third, a fourth, and finally a month had gone. I was growing sick with apprehension. What if something dreadful had happened and my lovely, only body was lying dead somewhere, too shattered for the fiend to remain longer within it, and gone for ever from me? What if the present occupant of my corse had again yielded to the seductive

THE CROWNING ACT OF INFAMY. 137

influence of the cup, and was off somewhere upon a prolonged spree? I floated uneasily in and about my quarters here, sleepless, worried to distraction. I searched my papers, as best I could without hands, to see if there was not some clue as to my whereabouts among them, and found none. I went through the contents of the waste basket even, and found nothing to relieve my dreadful anxiety, and then I went to the wardrobe to search the pockets of my clothes for possible evidence to calm my agitated soul.

"Toppleton, there was not one vestige of a garment in that clothes press from top to bottom. Not a shoe, not a coat, absolutely nothing. It was bare even as Mother Hubbard's cupboard was bare. This was an additional shock, and I became giddy with fear. I floated madly across to the bureau and peered into the drawers thereof. Beyond the ties I had formerly worn and the collars, frayed at the edges, of my negligée days, nothing remained, and then for the first time I noticed that my trunk was gone from the room.

"'What can it mean?' I asked myself, though I might as well have spared the question, for it was one I could not answer. Days came and went, leaving me still pondering. Christmas Eve came and found me here moping in a cheerless apartment, friendless, forlorn, clothesless and bodiless—a fine way to pass what should have been the happiest night of the year."

"Elegant!" said Toppleton. "It might have been worse though. If you had had your body and still been clothesless you would have found it rather cold, I fancy."

"I had almost given up all hope of ever seeing myself again," continued the exile, ignoring Hopkins' interruption, "when on the evening of January second I heard a step coming along the hall which I at once recognized as my own, my latch-key was inserted in the lock and the door was opened, and at last I stood before myself again, the picture of health and happiness.

"'Are you there?' my lips said with a broad smile, as my body entered the room.

"'I am,' I replied shortly; 'and I've been here, Heaven knows how long, worried sick to know what had become of you. I don't think you are the most considerate fiend in the world to take me off for weeks without letting me know anything of my whereabouts.'

"'I am very sorry,' said the fiend, throwing himself down on the lounge. 'I meant to have told you, but you were not here when I returned. Lord Smitherton invited me out to his house at Snorley Farms for the Christmas holidays along with the Earl of Pupley, General Carlingberry-Jimpson, and a half-dozen members of the Birmingham Society of Fine Arts. It was an invitation I could not well refuse, and, besides, our carcass here was beginning to feel the need of an outing, so I accepted. I came back here to tell you about it, but you must have been floating about somewhere else. At all events, you are much better for the outing, and your purely mortal self has had a good time. And, by the way, I want to warn you about one point. When you are the occupant of this corse, I think you would better not walk down Rotten Row, or go anywhere in fact where I am accustomed to going, because you don't know my friends any more than I know yours, and that is apt to lead to misunderstanding. Lady Romaine Cushing, who was visiting Lady Smitherton, told me that I had cut her dead in the Row one afternoon, although she had stopped her carriage particularly to speak to me. It was you who cut her, but, of course, you were not to blame, because you never saw Lady Romaine Cushing; but it is hard to explain away little matters of that sort, and I had the deuce of a time getting her to believe that her eye must have deceived her. We can't afford to offend our friends of the fair sex, you know; they can make or mar a man these days.'

"'And I am to be kept away from the haunts of polite society,' I said, with some natural indignation, 'just because it embarrasses *you* to explain why I don't bow to people I don't know.'

"'But it's all for your good,' he replied. 'You seem to forget that I am actuated entirely by the best of motives.'

"'No doubt,' I said, 'but I think it's rather hard on me to be excluded from the most attractive quarter of London.'

"'You are not excluded. You can walk there if you choose at night or very early in the morning, or when Society is out of town, or, better still, you can float there in your invisible state at any time. In fact,' added the fiend, ' it would be very enjoyable for you, I should think, to do that last. You can poise yourself over a tree for instance, and watch yourself hobnobbing with the illustrious. You can sit in your invisibility in any one of the carriages that roll to and fro, and, as long as you do not obtrude yourself on the occupants, there is not an equipage in London, high or low, in which you cannot ride. You are better off than I am in that respect. While I have no particular shape I am visible like a bit of sea-fog, but you being invisible can go anywhere without making trouble. The theatres are open to you free of charge. The best seats are at your disposal. If you choose to do it you could even sit on the throne of England, and nobody would be the wiser.'

"'That's all very well,' I said; 'but I don't care to travel about in that impersonal fashion. I prefer the incarnate manner of doing things, and if you will kindly permit me to assume bodily form once more, I'll be very much obliged.'

"'Certainly!' he replied, and with that we changed places.

"The sensation of getting back to my accustomed figure once more was delightful, and there was no denying the fact that I was better off for the outing I had so unceremoniously taken. My step was elastic, my head felt clear as a bell, and, altogether, I had never before enjoyed the consciousness of so great a physical strength as now was mine.

"This feeling gave me courage to do many things which I had hitherto put off, and among them was the making of a proposal of marriage to the admired Miss Hicksworthy-Johnstone. It was seven o'clock when the fiend had left me to the personal enjoyment of my complete self, and at eight o'clock I was in a hansom cab speeding out to the dwelling-place of the woman I loved. At eight thirty I was on my knees before her, and by eleven o'clock I was her accepted suitor. Such happiness as was mine, Hopkins, no man ever knew. The only trouble known to my soul at the moment was the consciousness that Arabella, as I was now permitted to call Miss Hicksworthy-Johnstone, was in the dark as to the methods by which my greatness had been achieved. I could not confess my dreadful secret to her, for that would have put an end entirely to our relations, and I loved her so that I could not bring myself to give her up. She asked me numberless questions of a most embarrassing sort, as if she suspected there was something wrong, but I managed in some way, I know not how, to give a plausible answer to every one of them."

"Possibly the fiend left a little of his brain in your head when he got out," suggested Toppleton.

"Perhaps so," returned the exile. "However it was, I managed to make out a satisfactory case for myself, and at the close of a cross-examination such as no man ever went through before, lasting two and a half hours, Arabella threw herself into my arms and called me by my first name. She was mine, and all the world seemed bright.

"I walked home," continued the spirit, "and in a condition of ecstasy that almost compensates for all I have suffered since. My feet seemed hardly to touch the ground, and I whistled from the time I left Arabella until I entered my room here,—a reprehensible habit, perhaps, but one which had always been my method of expressing satisfaction with the world. As I entered this room I was brought down from my ecstatic heights to an appreciation of my actual state, for the first thing to greet my eyes was the fiend, greener than ever, sitting by the fire ruminating apparently, for it was at least five minutes before he took note of my presence, although I addressed him politely as soon as I saw him.

"'Hallo,' he said finally. 'Where have you been?'

"The question was as unexpected as it was natural, and I was unprepared for it, so I made no reply, covering my silence by taking off my shoes and preparing for bed.

"'Where have you been?' he asked again, this time in a tone so peremptory that I decided in an instant not to tell him.

"'Out,' I answered. 'Where have you?'

"At this he laughed.

"'Don't be impudent,' he said. 'I do not wish to pry into your affairs. I only wanted to know where you had been because I am interested in you, and I want to help you to avoid pitfalls.'

"'That's all right,' I responded graciously. 'I appreciate your kindness, but you need not be interested in where I have been to-night, because I have been engaged in a little matter that concerns you not at all.'

"'Very well,' he replied, turning once more to the fire. 'I'll take your word for it; only you and I must be perfectly candid with each other, or complications may arise, that's all. By the way, I'll have to borrow you again to-morrow morning. There are a half-dozen members of Parliament coming here to discuss certain matters of state, and you would be somewhat embarrassed if you undertook to meet them.'

"'That suits me,' I said, happy enough to acquiesce in anything. 'Only I'll want to get back here to-morrow evening. I have an engagement.'

"The fiend eyed me narrowly for a moment, and I winced beneath his gaze.

"'All right,' he said, 'you can get back, but this Parliamentary business is very important, and I *must* have the semblance of a mortal being every morning this week.'

"'That can be arranged,' I replied. Arabella could have my evenings, and he could have my mornings. That was fair enough, I thought, and so it happened. Every night for a week I spent in the company of my *fiancée*,— whose name, by the way, I never mentioned in the fiend's presence—and every morning for the same period he was in charge, conducting negotiations which only served to make me more famous.

"Finally the dreadful morning came. It was Saturday, and the fiend and I were sitting together in my quarters. We had just changed places. I was in my present disembodied state, and the fiend had taken possession for the day, when there was heard in the corridor a quick nervous step which stopped as he who directed it came to my door, and a voice, which to my consternation I recognized at once as that of Arabella's father following close upon a resounding knock, cried out,—

"'This is the place. This is the kennel in which the hound lives. Open the door!'

"There was not time for the fiend and me to change places. Indeed, I had hardly recognized the old gentleman's voice, when the fiend in answer to his demand opened the door.

"A madder man than my prospective father-in-law appeared to be I never saw, Hopkins," said the spirit, his voice trembling with emotion. "He was livid, and when the door opened, and he saw the man he supposed to be me standing before him showing absolutely no signs of recognition, he fairly foamed at the mouth.

"'How do you do, sir?' said the fiend, polite as Chesterfield.

"'Don't speak to me, you puppy,' roared the old gentleman. "Don't you dare to address me until I address you.'

"'This is most extraordinary,' said the fiend, seemingly nonplussed at Mr. Hicksworthy-Johnstone's inexplicable wrath; for he could understand it no better than I, and to me it was absolutely incomprehensible, for I was not aware of anything that I had done that could possibly give rise to so violent an ebullition of rage. 'I am at a loss, sir, to understand why you enter the office of a gentleman in a fashion so unbecoming to one of your years; you must have made some mistake.'

"'Mistake!' shrieked Arabella's father. 'Mistake, you snivelling hypocrite? What mistake can there be? Do you see that note in this week's *Vanity Fair*, you vile deceiver? Do you see me? Do you see anything?'

"'I see you,' replied the fiend calmly, ' and I wish I didn't.'

"'I'll go bond you wish you didn't,' howled

the enraged visitor. 'And when I get through with you you'll wish I hadn't brought this oak stick along with me. Now I want to know what explanation you have to make of that paragraph in the paper.'

"'I cannot explain what I have not read,' returned the fiend. 'Nor shall I attempt to read what you wish to have explained until I know who you are, and what possible right you can have to demand an explanation of anything from me. What are you, anyhow, a retired maniac or simply an active imbecile?'

"As the fiend spoke these words," said the spirit, "I tried to arrest him; but he was so angry that he either could not or would not hear my whispered injunction that he be silent. As for the old gentleman, he sat gasping in his chair, glaring at my poor self, a perfect picture of apoplectic delirium. The fiend returned the glare unflinchingly.

"'Well!' gasped Mr. Hicksworthy-Johnstone after a minute's steady glance, 'if you aren't the coolest hand in Christendom. Who am I, eh? What am I here for, eh? What's my name, eh? What claim have I on you, eh? Young man, you are the most consummate Lothario on the footstool. You are a Don Juan with the hide of a rhinoceros and the calmness of a snow-clad Alp, but I can just tell you one thing. You can't trifle with Arabella!'

"And then, Hopkins, that infernal fiend looked my father-in law elect square in the eye and asked,—

"'Who the devil is Arabella?'

"As the words fell from my lips, the old gentleman with an oath started from his chair, and grasping the inkstand from the table, hurled it with all his force at my waistcoat, which received it with breathless surprise; and then, Toppleton, it breaks my heart to say it, but my foot—the foot of him who loved Arabella to distraction,—was lifted against her father, and the man to whom he had promised his daughter's hand, appeared to kick him forcibly, despite his grey hairs, out into and along the corridor to the head of the stairs. Then, as I watched, the two men grappled and went crashing down the stairs, head over heels together.

"Sick with fear and mortification, I flew back into the room, where, lying upon the floor, I saw the copy of *Vanity Fair* that Mr. Hicksworthy-Johnstone had brought, and marked with blue pencil upon the page before me was printed the announcement of the engagement of myself to Ariadne Maude, second daughter of John Edward Fackleton, Earl of Pupley, of Castle Marrowfat, Sauceton Downs, Worcestershire."

CHAPTER X.

THE SPIRIT'S STORY IS CONCLUDED.

"I SHOULD say," volunteered Hopkins, with a shake of his head, "that that was about the most unpleasant situation he had got you into yet; and yet he was not entirely to blame. He requested candour from you, and you declined to be candid. You should have told him of your engagement to Miss Hicksworthy-Johnstone. That would at least have prevented his kicking her father out of your office and rolling downstairs with him."

"It is easy enough to say now what ought to have been done," sobbed the exile. "I do not think you would have done very differently if you had been in my position. I was jealous of the fiend, I suppose, and I didn't know but what he would insist upon doing some of the courting—which would have been intolerable."

"Better that than to be set down by your

fiancée as a heartless trifler," returned Hopkins. "But what happened next? Was the old gentleman hurt?"

"Not he," replied the exile. "When he and I, as he supposed me to be, reached the bottom of the stairs he landed on top, and was the first to get on his feet again. And then, Hopkins, I was glad not to be in my normal condition; for as the fiend attempted to rise my Arabella's father, who still retained his grip upon that oak stick, gave me the worst licking I ever had in my life, and I—well, I really enjoyed the spectacle, because I knew that I deserved it. The fiend, hampered somewhat by the corse to which he was not yet entirely accustomed was at a tremendous disadvantage, and I know Mr. Hicksworthy-Johnstone's blows caused him considerable pain. The only possible escape for him was to leave the body, which he did just as the attacking party landed a resounding thwack upon the back of my neck. Of course, the minute the fiend evacuated the premises, I appeared to Mr. Hicksworthy-Johnstone to have been killed, because there was in reality no slightest bit of animation left in my body. It was the horror of this discovery that covered the retreat of the fiend, who, more horribly green than ever—the green that comes from rage—mounted the steps he had so summarily descended a moment before, and hurried into my room, dragging me by sheer force of will, which I was unable to resist, after him. You see, Hopkins, we were now nothing more than two consciousnesses; two minds, one mortal, the other immortal; one infinitely strong, the other finite in its limitations, and I was of course as powerless in the presence of the fiend as a babe in the arms of its nurse. Mr. Hicksworthy-Johnstone, thinking that he had killed me, after a vain endeavour to restore my stricken body to consciousness—in which he would have succeeded had the fiend permitted me to take possession again, for I did not wish Arabella's father to suppose for one instant that he was a murderer—sneaked on tip-toes from the building, and, mumbling to himself in an insane fashion, disappeared in the crowd of pedestrians on the street.

"'This is a pretty mess you've got us into,' said the fiend. 'I should like to know what excuse you can have for such infernal duplicity as you have been guilty of?'

"'I cannot discuss this matter with you,' I answered. 'The duplicity is not mine, but yours. You have endeavoured to exercise rights which were clearly not yours to exercise. I informed you that in matters of love—'

"'Matters of love!' he ejaculated. 'Do you

call this a matter of love? Do you think it's a matter of love for an entire stranger to throw a two-pound crystal inkstand loaded with ink at the very core of my waistcoat? Is it a matter of love for a grey-haired villain like that to drag me or you, whichever way you choose to put it, down a flight of stairs and then knock the life out of us? It seems to me, you have a strange idea of love.'

"'Don't you understand!' I cried. 'That man was only doing his duty. He is Arabella's father!'

"'Again, I must ask,' said the fiend, in a manner that aggravated me as it had aggravated the old gentleman, 'who, in all creation, is Arabella?'

"'My *fiancée!*' I yelled. 'My *fiancée*, you poor blind omniscient! Whom did you suppose?'

"As I uttered these words, Hopkins, the fiend's whole manner changed. He was no longer flustered and angry merely; he was a determined and very angry being. He rose from his chair, and fixing his eye upon the point where he thought I was—and he had a faculty of establishing that point accurately at all times—and pointing that horrible finger of his at me, fairly hissed with rage.

"'That settles it, sir,' he cried. 'You and

I part for ever. You, by your foolish perversity, by your inexplicable lack of candour, by your sinful refusal to trust your welfare to my hands, who have done so much for you, have nearly overthrown the whole structure of the greatness I have builded up. Your idiotic behaviour has decided me to do that which from the very beginning I have most feared. I have been haunted by the fear that you would want to marry some woman simply for the empty, mortal reason that you loved her, utterly ignoring the fact that by a judicious matrimonial step you could attain to heights that otherwise could never be yours. Having your interests entirely in view, I had arranged a match which would strengthen into permanence your, at present, rather uncertain hold upon society. Lady Ariadne Maude Fackleton, to whom you are at present engaged, as the daughter of the Earl of Pupley, can give you the *entrée* to the best circles in London or out of it; while this Arabella of yours can serve only to assist you in spending your income and keeping your parlour free from dust. Now, what earthly use was there in your philandering—'

"'I fancy I have a right to select my own wife,' I said.

"'You always were strong on fancies,' he

retorted. 'You might have known that with the career opening up before you a plain Arabella would never do. Do you suppose you could take her to a ball at the Earl of Mawlberry's? Do you suppose that any woman, in fact, who would consent to marry you as your weak inefficient self could go anywhere and do me justice? I guess not; and your behaviour has settled our partnership for ever. We part for good.'

"'Well, I'm glad of it,' I retorted, goaded to anger by his words. 'Get out. I don't want to see you again. You've ruined me by putting me in false positions from the time we met until now, and I am sick of it. You can't leave too soon to suit me.'

"When I had spoken these words he darted one final venomous glance at me, and walked whistling from the room. As long as his whistle was perceptible I remained quiet—quiet as my agitation would permit; and then, when the last flute-like note died away in the distance, I floated from the room and down the stairs to get my poor bruised body and put it in shape to call on Arabella.

"Hopkins, when I reached the foot of the stairs my body had disappeared! I was frantic with fear. I did not know whether it had been found by the janitor and conveyed to the morgue, whether Arabella's father had returned to conceal it, and so conceal his fancied crime, or whether the fiend had finally crowned his infamous work by stealing it. I sought for it in vain. Forgetful of my invisibility, I asked the janitor if he had seen it, and he fled shrieking with fear from the building, and declined ever thereafter to enter it again. Every nook and corner in the Temple I searched and found it not, and then I floated dejectedly to Arabella's home, where I found her embracing her father in a last fond farewell. The old gentleman was about leaving the country to escape the consequences of his crime.

"'Arabella!' I cried, as I entered the room.

"The girl turned a deadly white, and her father fell cringing upon his knees, and then I realized that, recognizing my voice, they feared my ghost had come to haunt them, and with this realization came to my consciousness the overwhelming thought that both would go insane were I to persist in speaking while invisible.

"The situation, Hopkins, was absolutely terrible, and if I had had my teeth I should have gnashed them for the very helplessness of my condition."

"Did the old gentleman persist in his

determination to leave the country?" asked Hopkins.

"He did. He sailed for the United States on a small freight schooner that night, and reached New York in time to hear in that far-off clime of the marriage of his supposed victim; but I must not anticipate," said the exile.

"For three weeks after that horrible day I never caught sight of my missing person, nor did I discover the slightest clue as to its whereabouts. It never turned up at my quarters that I could learn, but that it was not dead or buried I had good reason to believe; for one morning, while I was away from my rooms floating along Rotten Row, hoping to catch sight of myself if perchance I still lived, four truckmen arrived at the Temple here and moved all my clothes and furniture, whither I never discovered, in consequence of which act, upon my return here, I found the room cold and bare as a barn."

"That was rank robbery," said Toppleton.

"We should have trouble in establishing that fact in court," returned the exile. "I could not deny on oath that my hand had penned the order for the removal of the goods, and as for the clothes and other things, most of them had been bought by the money I had earned through the fiend's instrumentality."

"That is so," said Toppleton, hastily acquiescing in the exile's words, lest he should seem to his visitor less acute than a full-fledged lawyer should be. "And how long was it before you encountered yourself once more?"

"Three weeks," returned the exile. "And where do you suppose the meeting took place?"

"I don't know," said Hopkins. "At Buckingham Palace?"

"No, sir. In Arabella's parlour! It was just three weeks from the hour in which Mr. Hicksworthy-Johnstone appeared at my office door in the Temple that, for the want of something better to do, I floated into Arabella's parlour again, and was filled with consternation to see standing there before the mirror, adjusting his tie, the fiend in full possession of my treasured self. I was about to utter a cry of delight when I heard an ejaculation of fear behind me, and turning saw Arabella herself entering the room, pale as a sheet. I tell you Hopkins, it was dramatic; though, as far as the fiend was concerned, he was as nonchalant as could be.

"'You are not dead!' cried Arabella, hoarsely.

"'Not that I am aware of, madam,' said the fiend coolly. 'Have I the honour of addressing Miss Arabella Hicksworthy-Johnstone?'

"'Oh, Edward, Edward,' she cried—'I forgot to tell you, Hopkins,' explained the spirit, 'my name was Edward'—'oh, Edward, what does this mean?' she cried. 'My father has fled to America, thinking that in that unhappy moment of Saturday three weeks ago he had killed you.'

"'Indeed!' returned the fiend. 'I sincerely hope he will enjoy the trip, though he did inflict injuries upon me from which I shall be a long time in recovering. But tell me, madame, are you Miss Arabella Hicksworthy-Johnstone?'

"'Edward,' she replied, 'are you mad?'

"'I have a right to be indignant at your father's treatment of me, if that vilely vindictive old person was your father, but I am not what you might call mad. I cherish no vindictive feelings. But as my time is limited I should like to proceed at once to the business I have in hand, if you will permit me.'

"Arabella sat aghast as the man she deemed her *fiancé* spoke these words to her. She was utterly unable to comprehend the situation, and I could not clarify the cloud upon her understanding without imperilling her reason.

Oh, Hopkins, Hopkins, were the fires of Hades to become extinguished to-day, there are other tortures for the spirit close at hand more hideously unbearable even than they!"

"It would seem so," said Hopkins. "If I had my choice between your experience and Hades, I think I should warm up to the latter. But go on. What did Arabella say?"

"She drew herself up proudly after a moment of hesitation, and said, 'I have no desire to hinder you in going about your business.'

"'Thanks,' said the fiend. 'Assuming that you are Miss Arabella Hicksworthy-Johnstone, I would say to you that I should like to know upon what your father's claim that you and I are engaged rests.'

"'Really, Edward,' she returned impatiently, 'I cannot comprehend your singular behaviour this afternoon. You know how we became engaged. You know you asked me to be your wife, and you know that after keeping you on your knees for several hours I consented.'

"'Madam,' observed the fiend, 'I never went on my knees to a woman in my life. I never asked but one woman in this world to be my wife, and you are not she.'

"'What!' cried Arabella. 'Do you mean to say to me, Edward, that you did *not* ask me to be your wife?'

"'I meant to say exactly what I said. That I am engaged to be married to Lady Ariadne Maude Fackleton, daughter of the Earl of Pupley, the only woman to whom I ever spoke or thought of speaking a word of love in my life. I mean to say that Lady Ariadne Maude Fackleton and I expect to be married before the month is up. I mean to say that I never saw you before in my life, and I should like to know what your intentions are concerning this absurd claim that I am engaged to you may be, for I do not intend to have my future marred by any breach of promise suits. In short, madam, do you intend to claim me as your matrimonial prize or not? If not, all well and good. If so, I shall secure an injunction restraining you from doing anything of the sort. Even should you force me to the altar itself I should then and there forbid the banns.'

"'Sir,' said my Arabella, drawing herself up like a queen, 'you may leave this house, and never set foot again within its walls. I should as soon think of claiming that celebrated biblical personage, of whom you remind me, Ananias, for a husband as you. Do not flatter yourself that I shall ever dispute the Lady Ariadne's possession of so accomplished a lord and master as yourself,—though I should do so were I more philanthropically disposed. If it be the duty of one woman to protect the happiness of another, I should do all that lies in my power to prevent this marriage; but inasmuch as my motive in so doing would, in all likelihood, be misconstrued, I must abstain; I must hold myself aloof, though the whole future happiness of one of my own sex be at stake. Farewell, sir, and good riddance. If you will leave me Lady Ariadne's address, I will send her my sympathy as a wedding gift.'

"'Madam,' returned the fiend, bowing low, 'your kind words have taken a heavy load from my heart. You deserve a better fate; but farewell.'

"Then as the fiend departed Arabella swooned away. My first impulse was to follow the fiend, and to discover if possible his address; but I could not bring myself to leave Arabella at that moment, she was so overcome. I floated to the prostrate woman, and whispered the love I felt for her in her ear.

"'Arabella,' I said. 'Arabella—my love—it is all a mistake. Open your eyes and see. I am here ready to explain all if you will only listen.'

"Her answer was a moan and a fluttering of the eyelids.

"'Arabella,' I repeated. 'Don't you hear

me, sweetheart? Open your eyes and look at me. It is I, Edward.'

"' Edward!' she gasped, her eyes still closed. 'What *does* it all mean? Why have you treated me so?'

"' It is not I who have done this Arabella; it is another vile being over whose actions I have no control. He is a fiend who has me in his power. He is—oh, Arabella, do not ask me, do not insist upon knowing all, only believe that I am not to blame!'

"' Kiss me, Edward,' she murmured. 'One little kiss.'

"Hopkins," moaned the exile, "just think of that! One little kiss was all she asked, and I—I hadn't anything to kiss her with—not the vestige of a lip.

"' Kiss me, Edward,' she repeated.

"' I cannot,' I cried out in anguish.

"' Why not?' she demanded, sitting up on the floor and gazing wildly around her, and then seeing that she was absolutely alone in the room, and had been conversing with—"

"Oh!" ejaculated Hopkins, wringing his hands. "Dear me! The poor girl must have been nearly crazy."

"Nearly, Hopkins?" said the exile, in a sepulchral tone. "Nearly? Arabella never did anything by halves or by nearlies. She became quite crazy, and as far as I know has remained so until this day, for with the restoration of consciousness, and the shock of opening her eyes to see nothing that could speak with her, and yet had spoken, her mind gave way, and she fled chattering like an imbecile from the room. I have never seen her since!"

"And the fiend?" queried Toppleton.

"I saw him at St. George's on the following Wednesday," returned the exile. "I had been wandering aimlessly and distractedly about London for four days since the dreadful episode at Arabella's, when I came to St. George's Church. There was an awning before the door, and from the handsome equipages drawn up before the edifice I knew that some notable function was going on within. The crowds, the usual London crowds, were being kept back by the police, but I, of course, being invisible, floated over their heads, past the guards, through the awning into the church. There was a wedding in progress, and the groom's back seemed familiar, though I could not place it at first, and naturally, Toppleton, for it was my own, as I discovered, a moment later. When the last irrevocable words binding me to a woman I had never before seen had been spoken, and the organ began to peal forth the melodious measures of the Lohengrin

March, the bride and groom, made one, turned and faced the brilliant assemblage of guests, among whom were the premier and the members of his cabinet, and as complete a set of nabobs, mentioned in Burke, as could be gathered in London at that time of the year, and I recognized my own face wreathed in smiles, my own body dressed in wedding garb, standing on the chancel steps ready to descend.

"I was married, Hopkins, at last. Married to a woman of beauty and wealth and high position, utterly unknown to me, and not only were my own mother and my best friends absent, but I myself had only happened in by accident.

"My rage knew no bounds, and as the fiend and his bride passed down the aisle amid the showered congratulations of the aristocratic multitude, I impotently endeavoured to strike him, of which he was serenely unconscious; but as he left the church my voice, which had been stifled with indignation, at last grew clear, and I howled out high above the crowds,—

"'You vile scoundrel, restore me to myself! Give me back the presence of which you have robbed me, or may every curse in all the universe fall upon you and your house for ever.'

"He heard me, Toppleton, and his answer

was a smile—a green smile—seeing which his bride, the Lady Ariadne Maude Fackleton, fainted as they drove away.

"That, Hopkins, is substantially the tale of villainy I have come to tell. Little remains to be told. The fiend has been true to his promise to make me famous, for every passing year has brought some new honour to my name. I have been elevated to the peerage; I have been ambassador to the most brilliant courts of Europe; I have been all that one could hope to be, and yet I have not been myself. I ask your assistance. Will you not give it to me?"

"Edward," said Toppleton warmly, "I will. I will be candid with you, Edward. I am almost as ignorant of law as a justice of the peace, but for your sake I will study and see what can be done. I will fight your case for you to the very last, but first tell me one thing. Your name is what?'

"Edward Pompton Chatford."

"What!" cried Toppleton, "the famous novelist?"

"He made me so," said the exile.

"And the fiend's present title is?"

"Lord Barncastle of Burningford."

"He?" said Toppleton, incredulously, recognizing the name as that of one who fairly bent beneath the honours of the world.

"None other," returned the exile.

"Heavens!" ejaculated Toppleton. "How Morley, Harkins, Perkins, Mawson, Bronson, Smithers, and Hicks will open their eyes when I tell them that I have been retained to institute *habeas corpus* proceedings in the case of Chatford *v.* Barncastle of Burningford! Morley, particularly, I am afraid will die of fright!"

CHAPTER XI.

TOPPLETON CONSULTS THE LAW AND FORMS AN OPINION.

AT the conclusion of the exile's story Hopkins glanced at his watch, and discovered that he had barely time to return to his lodging and dress for a little dinner he had promised to attend that evening.

" I will look up the law in this case of yours, Chatford," he said, rising from his chair and putting on his hat and coat, "and in about a week I rather think we shall be able to decide upon some definite line of action. It will be difficult, I am afraid, to find any precedent to guide us in a delicate matter of this sort, but as a lay lawyer, if I may be allowed the expression, it seems to me that there ought to be some redress for one who has been made the victim of so many different kinds of infamy at once as you have. The weak part of our case is that you were yourself an accessory to every single one of the fiend's crimes, and in instituting a suit at law we cannot get around the fact that in a measure you are both plaintiff and defendant. I believe those are the terms usually employed to designate the two parties to a suit, except in the case of an appeal, when there is an appellant and a repellant if my memory serves me."

"It may be as you say," returned the exile, sadly. "I'll have to take your word for it entirely, since, as I have already told you, all the law I ever knew I have forgotten, and then, too, my business being purely one of adjudication, I used to distinguish my clients one from another—representing, as I did, both sides—by calling them, respectively, the compromisee and the compromisor."

"Well," Toppleton said, "I'll find out all about it and let you know, say, by Friday next. We'll first have to decide in what capacity you shall appear in court, whether as a plaintiff or defendant. I think under the circumstances you will have to go as a plaintiff, though in a case in which my father was interested some years ago, I know that it was really the plaintiff who was put on the defensive as soon as the old gentleman took him in hand to cross-examine him. It was said by experts to have been the crossest examination on the calendar that year; and between you and me, Edward, the plaintiff never forgave his attorneys for not retaining the governor on his side in the beginning. If you would rather go as a defendant, I suppose I could arrange to have it so, but it strikes me as a disadvantageous thing to do in these days, because in most cases, it is the defendant who has committed the wrong upon which the suit is based, and a man who starts in as the underdog, has to combat the prejudices of judge, jury and general public, with whom it is a time-honoured custom to believe a man guilty until he has proven his innocence. I think, on the whole, it would be easier for you to prove Lord Barncastle's guilt than your own innocence."

"I know from the lucid manner in which you talk, Toppleton," said the exile, with a deep sigh indicating satisfaction, "from the readiness and extemporaneousness with which you grasp the situation, not losing sight of side issues, that I have made no mistake in coming to you. Heaven bless you, sir. You will never regret the assistance you are so nobly giving to one you have never seen."

"Don't mention it, Sallie—I should say Chatford," said Toppleton. "I am an American citizen and will ever be found championing the cause of the oppressed against the oppressor. My ears are ever open to the plaint of the plaintiff, nor shall I be deaf to the defendant in case you choose to be the latter. Count on me, Edward, and all will yet be well!"

With these inspiring words, Toppleton lit his cigar and walked jauntily from the room, and the exile relapsed into silence.

Faithful to his promise, Toppleton applied himself assiduously to the study of the law as it seemed to him to bear upon the case of his mysterious client. To be sure, his library was not quite as extensive as it might have been, and there may have been points in other books than the ones he had, which would have affected his case materially, but the young lawyer was more or less self-reliant, and what he had to read he read intelligently.

"If I were called upon suddenly to rescue a young woman from drowning, and possessed nothing but an anchor and a capstan bar to do it with, my duty clearly would be to do the best I could with those tools, however awkward they might be. I could not ease my conscience after neglecting to do all that I could with those tools, by saying that I hadn't a lifeboat and a cork suit handy. Here is a parallel case. I must do the best I can with the tools I have, and I guess I can find enough law in Blackstone and that tree calf copy of the sixteenth volume of Abbott's 'Digest' I picked up the other day to cover this case. If I can't, I'll have to use the sense that Nature gave me, and go ahead anyhow."

To his delight, Hopkins found it utterly unnecessary for him to read the tree calf sixteenth volume of Abbott's " Digest," he found so much in the " Comic Blackstone " that applied.

" Why, do you know," he said to the exile when they met, the one to explain the law, the other to listen, " do you know you have the finest case in all Christendom, without leaving the very fundamental principles of the law? It's really extraordinary what a case you have, or rather, would have, if you could devise some means of appearing in court. That's the uncrackable nut in the case. How the deuce to have you appear on the witness stand, I can't see. The court would not tolerate any such makeshift as the Aunt Sallie scheme you and I have adopted, it would be so manifestly absurd, and would give the counsel for the defence— for you must be the plaintiff after all, can't help yourself—it would give the counsel for the defence the finest chance to annihilate us by the use of his satirical powers he had ever had, and before a jury that would simply ruin our cause at the outset."

" I don't see why I can't testify as I am— bodiless as I have been left. The mere absence of my body and presence of my consciousness would almost prove my case," said the exile.

"It would seem as if it ought to," said Toppleton. "But you know what men are. They believe very little that they hear, and not much more than half that they see. You couldn't expect anyone to believe the points of a person unseen. If they can't see you they can't see your hardships, and besides, hearsay evidence unsupported is not worth shucks."

"I don't know what shucks are," returned the exile, "but I see your point."

"It's a serious point," said Toppleton. "And then there is another most embarrassing side to it. We can't afford to have our case weakened by putting ourselves in a position where countercharges can be brought against us, and I am very much afraid our opponents would charge vagrancy against you, for the very obvious and irrefutable reason that you have absolutely no visible means of support. You wouldn't have a leg to stand on if they did that, and yet it does seem a pity that something cannot be done to enable you to appear, for as I said a minute ago, you have otherwise a perfectly magnificent cause of action. Why, Edward, there isn't a page in the Comic Blackstone that does not contain something that applies to your case, and that ought to make you a winner if we could get around this horrible lack of body of yours.

"For instance," continued Toppleton, opening A'Beckett's famous contribution to legal lore, "in the very first chapter we find that Blackstone divides rights into rights of *persons* and rights of things. Clearly you have a right to your own person, and no judge on a sane bench would dare deny it. Absolute rights, it says here, belong to man in a state of nature, which being so, you have been wronged, because in being deprived of your state of nature you have been robbed of your absolute rights. Clear as crystal, eh?"

"That's so," said the exile. "You are a marvel at law, Hopkins."

"In section six reference is made to the *habeas corpus* act of Charles the Second, and unless I have forgotten my Latin, that is a distinct reference to a man's right to the possession of his own body. Section eight, same chapter, announces man's right to personal security, and asserts his legal claim to the enjoyment of *life, limbs, health and reputation.* Have you enjoyed your life? No! Have you enjoyed your limbs? Not for thirty years. Have you enjoyed your health. No! Barncastle of Burningford has enjoyed that as well as your reputation. I think on the whole though, we would better not say anything about your reputation if we get into court, for while it is undoubtedly *yours*, and has been by no means enjoyed by you, you didn't make it for yourself. That was his work, and he is entitled to it."

"True," said the exile. "I do not wish to claim anything I am not entitled to."

"That's the proper spirit," said Toppleton. "You want what belongs to you and nothing more. You are entitled to your property, for which section eleven of this same chapter provides, saying that the law will not allow a man to be deprived of his property except by the law itself. If a man's own body isn't his, I'd like to know to whom it belongs in a country that professes to be free!"

Toppleton paused at this point to make a few notes and to reinforce his own spirit by means of others.

"Now, under the head of real property, Chatford," he said, "I find that in England property is real or personal. I think that in this case, that of which you have been deprived comes under both heads. One's body is certainly real and unquestionably personal, and if a man has a right to the possession of each, he has a right to the possession of both, and he who robs him of both is guilty of a crime under each head. Real property consists of lands, tenements and hereditaments. Lands we must perforce exclude because you have lost no lands. Tenements may be alluded to, however, with absolute fairness because the body is the tenement of the soul. Of hereditaments I am not sure. I don't know what hereditaments are, and I haven't had time to find out anything about them except that they are corporeal or incorporeal, which leads me to infer that you have been wronged under this head also, for I must assume that a hereditament is something that may or may not have a body according to circumstances, which is your case exactly.

"Now a man's right to the possession of an estate is called his title, if I am not mistaken," continued Hopkins, "and it is only reasonable to suppose that this refers to bodily estate as well as to landed estate. What we must dispute is Barncastle's title to your bodily estate. Our case is referred to in section two, chapter nine, part second of this book, which deals with joint tenancy in which two or more persons have one and the same interest in an estate, but it must be held by both at the same time. Now, even granting, as the other side may say, that you entered into a partnership with the fiend, we could knock him right off his pins on the sole fact that in declining to admit you to your own bodily estate, he has not only deprived you of an undoubted right, but has in reality forfeited his own claim to possession, since he has violated the only principle of law upon which he could claim entrance to the estate under any circumstances."

"Superb!" ejaculated the exile.

"Now we come to an apparent difficulty," continued Hopkins. "Possession is, according to my authority, five points of the law. The fiend has possession, and in consequence tallies five points; out of how many I do not know. What the maximum number of points in the law is, the book does not say, but even assuming that they form a good half, I think we can bring forward five more with a dozen substitutes for each of the five in support of our position. Some of these points will evolve themselves when we come to consider whence Barncastle's title was derived.

"Did he acquire his title by descent? No; unless it was by a descent to unworthy tricks which, I fear, are outside of the meaning of the law. By purchase? If so, let him show a receipt. By occupancy? Yes, and by a forcible occupancy which was as justifiable as his occupation of the throne would be, an occupancy which can be shown in court to be an entire subversion of the right of a prior occupant whose title was acquired by inheritance."

"That's a stong point," said the exile.

"Yes, it is," said Hopkins, "especially in a country where birth means so much. But that isn't all we have to say on this question of title. A title can be held by prescription. Barncastle may claim that he got his this way, but we can meet that by showing that he compounded his own prescription, and originally got you to swallow it by a trick. He also has a title by alienation, and there I think we may be weak since you were a party to the final alienation, though we may be able to pull through on even that point by showing that you consented only in the expectation of an early return of the premises. It was an alienation by deed, an innocent deed on your part, an infamous one on his. It was not an alienation of record, which weakens his claim, but one of special custom, which by no means weakens yours.

"And so, Edward, we might go on through the whole subject of the right of property, and on every point we are strong, and on few can Barncastle of Burningford put in the semblance of a defence."

"It's simply glorious," said the exile. "I don't believe there ever was a case like it."

"I don't believe so either," said Toppleton.

"And on the whole I'm glad there never was. I should hate to think that a crime like this could ever become a common one.

"Now," he said, resuming the discussion of the legal aspect of the exile's case, "let us see what we can find under the head of ' Private and Public Wrongs and their Remedies!' I suppose yours would come under the head of a civil wrong, though your treatment has been very far from civil. As such your redress lies in the Courts. You are forbidden to take back what has been taken from you by a force which amounts to a breach of the peace,—that is, it would not be lawful for you to seize your own body and shake the life out of it for the purpose of yourself becoming once more its animating spirit.

"First we must decide, ' What is the wrong that has been put upon you?' Well, it's almost any crime you can think of. He has dispossessed you of that which is yours. He has ousted you from your freehold. He has been guilty of trespass. He has subjected you to a nuisance, that is if it is a nuisance to be deprived of one's body, and I should think it would so appear to any sane person. He has been guilty of subtraction. He has subtracted you from your body and your body from you, leaving apparently no remainder. He has been guilty of an offence against your religion. To an extent he has committed an offence against the public health in that he has haunted citizens of this city and caused you unwittingly to do the same to the detriment of the sanity of those who have been haunted. I think we might even charge him with homicide, for if depriving a man of thirty years of his corporeal existence isn't depriving him of life, I don't know what is. However this may be, I am convinced that he is guilty of mayhem, for he certainly has deprived you of a limb—that is shown by your utter absence of limb. He has been guilty of an offence against your habitation, corporeal and incorporeal, and finally he has been guilty of larceny both grand and petty. Grand in the extent of it, petty in the method. By Jove, Chatford, if we could bring you into Court as a concrete individual, and not as an abstract entity, we could get up an indictment against Lord Barncastle of Burningford that would quash him for ever.

" A body obtained for you, I should carry the case to the Appellate Court at once, for two reasons. First because it would not be appropriate to try so uncommon a cause in the Common Pleas, second because a decision by the Court of Appeals is final, and we should save time by going there at once; but the point with which we must concern ourselves the most is, how shall we bring you before the eyes of the court; how shall we get our plaintiff into shape—visible shape?"

A painful silence followed the conclusion of Toppleton's discussion of the law in the case of Chatford *v.* Barncastle of Burningford. It was evident that the exile could think of no means of surmounting the unfortunate barrier to a successful prosecution of the case. Finally the exile spoke :

"I perceive the dreadful truth of what you say. Having no physical being, I have no standing in court."

"That's the unfortunate fact," returned Hopkins. "Can't you get a body in some way? Can't you borrow one temporarily?"

"Where?" asked the exile. "You are my only material friend. You wouldn't lend me yours."

"No, I wouldn't," said Toppleton. "If I did, where would your only material friend be? It's hopeless, Edward; and now that I think of it, even if you did get a form and should go to court, where are your witnesses? You could only assert, and Barncastle could always deny. Strong as your cause is, the courts, under the circumstances, will give you no redress, because you cannot prove your case. We must seek other means; this is a case that requires diplomatic action. Strategy will do more for us than law, and I think I have a scheme."

"Which is?"

"I will go to Lord Barncastle, and by means of a little clever dissembling will frighten him into doing the right thing by you. I realize what a tremendous undertaking it is, but failure then would not mean public disgrace, and failure in the courts would put us, and particularly myself, under a cloud. In short, we might be suspected of blackmail, Chatford; Barncastle is so prominent, and liable to just such attacks at all times."

"But how do you propose to reach him? He has the reputation now of being the haughtiest and most unapproachable member of the aristocracy."

"Oh, dear!" laughed Hopkins. "You don't understand Americans. Why, Chatford, we can push ourselves in anywhere. If you were a being like myself, and had ten pounds to bet, I would wager you that within forty-eight hours I could have an invitation in autograph from the Prince of Wales himself to dine with him and Prince Battenburg at Sandringham, at any hour, and on any day I choose to set. You don't know what enterprising fellows we Yankees are. I'll know Lord Barncastle intimately inside of one month, if I once set out to do it."

"Excuse me for saying it, Hopkins," said the exile, sadly, "but I must say that what I have liked about you in the past has been your freedom from bluster and brag. To me these statements of yours sound vain and empty. I would speak less plainly were it not that my whole future is in your hands, and I do not want you to imperil my chances by rashness. Tell me how you propose to meet Barncastle, and, having met him, what you propose to do, if you do not wish me to set this talk down as foolish braggadocio."

"I'll tell you how I propose to meet him," said Hopkins, slightly offended, and yet characteristically forgiving; "but what I shall do after that I shall not tell you, for I may find that he is a politer person than you are, and it's just possible that I shall like him. If I do, I may be impelled to desert you and ally myself with him. I don't like to be called a braggart, Edward."

"Forgive me, Hopkins," said the spirit. "I am so wrought up by my hopes and fears, by the consciousness of the terrible wrongs I have suffered, that I hardly know what I am saying."

"Well, never mind," rejoined Hopkins.

"Don't worry. The chances of my deserting you are very slight. But to return to your question. I shall meet Barncastle in this way; I shall have a sonnet written in his praise by an intimate friend of mine, a poet of very high standing and little morality, which I shall sign with my own name, and have printed as though it were a clipping from some periodical. This clipping I will send to Lord Barncastle with a note telling him that I am an American admirer of his genius, the author of the sonnet, and have but one ambition, which I travelled from America to gratify—to meet him face to face."

"Aha!" said the spirit. "An appeal to his vanity, eh?"

"Precisely," said Toppleton. "It works every time."

"And when you meet him?"

"We shall see," rejoined Toppleton. "I have given up brag and bluster; but if Lord Barncastle of Burningford does not take an interest in Hopkins Toppleton after he has known him fifteen minutes, I'll go back home to New York, give up my law practice and become—"

"What?" said the spirit as Hopkins hesitated.

"A sister of charity," said Hopkins, gravely.

CHAPTER XII.

TOPPLETON MAKES A FAIR START.

A FEW weeks later Toppleton was able to report progress to his invisible client. He had the sonnet to Barncastle of Burningford and was much pleased with it, because, in spite of the fact that it was two lines too long, he was confident that it would prove very fetching to the man to whom it was addressed.

"You ought to take out those two extra lines, though," said the exile. "Barncastle is a great stickler for form, and he will be antagonized at once by your violation of the rules."

"Not a bit of it," returned Toppleton. "Those lines stay right there, and I'll tell you why. In the first place Barncastle, as an Englishman, will see in the imperfect sonnet something that will strike him as a bit of American audacity, which will be very pleasing to him, and will give him something to talk about. As a Briton you are probably aware that your countrymen are very fond of discovering outrages of that sort in the work of those over the sea, because it is a sort of convincing proof that the American as a writer is still an inferior, and that England's controlling interest in the Temple of Immortality is in no danger of passing into alien hands. In the second place, he will be so pleased with the extra amount of flattery that is crammed into those two lines that he will not have the heart to criticize them; and thirdly, as one who knows it all, he will be prompted to send for me to come to him, in order that he may point out to me in a friendly spirit one or two little imperfections in what he will call my otherwise exquisite verse. I tell you what it is, Edward," said Toppleton, pausing a moment, " I never devoted myself with any particular assiduity to Latin, Greek, or mathematics, but when it comes to human nature, I am, as we New Yorkers say, a daisy, which means that I am the flower upon which you may safely bet as against the field."

"You certainly have an ingenious mind, Hopkins," returned the exile, "and I hope it will all go as you say, but I fear, Hopkins, I fear."

"Wait and see," was Hopkins' confident

reply, and being unable to do otherwise the exile obeyed.

In three days the sonnet was printed, and so fixed that it appeared to be a clipping from the *Rocky Mountain Quarterly Review, a Monthly Magazine.*

"That'll strike him as another interesting Americanism," said Hopkins, with a chuckle. "There is no people on earth but my own who would dare publish a quarterly twelve times a year."

To the sonnet was appended the name "Hopkins Parkerberry Toppleton;" Parkerberry being a novelty introduced into the signature by the young lawyer, not because he was at all entitled to it, but for the proper reason, as he said, that no American poet was worth a nickel who hadn't three sections to his name. A note with a distinctly western flavour to it was penned, and with the "decoy" sonnet went that night to Burningford Castle addressed to "His Excellency, Lord Barncastle," and then Toppleton and the exile sat down to await the result.

They had not many days to wait, for within a week of the dispatch of the poem and the note Hopkins, on reaching the office one morning, found the exile in a great state of excitement over a square envelope lying on the floor immediately under the letter slot Hopkins had had made in the door.

"It's come, Hopkins, it's come!" cried the exile.

"What's come?" queried Hopkins, calmly.

"The letter from Barncastle. I recognize my handwriting. It came last night about five minutes after you left the office, and I have been in a fever of excitement to learn its contents ever since. Do open it at once. What does he say?"

"Be patient, Edward, don't get so excited. Suppose you were to have an apoplectic stroke!"

"I can't be patient, and I can't have apoplexy, so do hurry. What do I say?"

"Seems to me," returned Hopkins, picking up the letter and slowly opening it, "it seems to me you are getting confused. But let's see; what *does* Barncastle say? H'm!" he said, reading the note. "'Barncastle Hall, Fenwick Morton, Mascottonton-on-the-Barbundle, December 19th, 189—. Hopkins Parkerberry Toppleton, Esquire, 17, Temple, London. Dear Sir,—I have to thank you for your favour and enclosure of the 13th inst. Your sonnet is but one of a thousand gratifying evidences I am daily receiving that I have managed to win to no inconsiderable degree the good will of your countrymen. It is also evidence to me that you are a young man of much talent in the line of original versification, since, apart from the sentiment you express, your sonnet is one of the most original I have ever seen, not only for its length, but also for the wonderful mixture of your metaphor. It is truly characteristic of your great and growing country, and I cannot resist your naïve appeal to be permitted to meet the unworthy object of its praise. I should be gratified to have you to dinner at Barncastle Hall, at eight o'clock on the evening of December 23rd, 189—. Kindly inform me by return post if your engagements will permit us to have the pleasure of having you with us on that evening. Believe me to be, with sentiments of regard, ever, my dear sir, faithfully yours, BARNCASTLE.'"

"By heavens!" ejaculated the exile, in delighted accents, "you've got there, Hopkins, you've got there. You'll go, of course?"

"Well, rather," returned Toppleton; "and to carry out the illusion, as well as to pique his interest in America, I'll wear a blue dress coat. But first let me reply."

"Dear Barncastle," he wrote. "I'll be there. Yours for keeps,—TOPPLETON."

"How's that?" he asked, reading it aloud to the exile.

TOPPLETON MAKES A FAIR START. 189

"You're not going to send that, are you?" said the exile in disgust.

"I'm not, eh? Well just you watch me and see," said Toppleton. "Why, Edward, that will be the biggest *coup* of the lot. He will get that letter, and he will be amused by it, and the more he thinks of it the more he'll like it, and then he'll say to himself, 'why, this man is a character;' and then do you know what will happen, Chatford?"

"I'll be hanged if I do," growled the exile.

"Well, I'll tell you. He will invite all the high panjandrums he knows to that dinner to meet me, and he will tell them that I am an original, and they'll all come, Chatford, just as they would flock to see a seven-humped camel or a dwarf eight feet high, and then I will have Lord Barncastle of Burningford just where I want him. I could browbeat him for weeks alone and never frighten him, but once I let him know that I know his secret, in the presence of his wife and a brilliant company, *he* will be apprehensive, and, if I mistake not, will be more or less within my reach."

"Lady Barncastle is no longer living," said the exile. "His household is presided over by his daughter."

"Very well," said Hopkins. "We'll dazzle the daughter too."

"Is this the way American lawyers do business generally?" sneered the exile.

"No," returned Toppleton; "there is probably not another American lawyer who would take a case like yours. That's the one respect in which they resemble your English lawyers, but I'll tell you one thing. When they start in to do a thing they do it, unless their clients get too fresh, and then they stop *in medias res.*"

"I hope there is nothing personal in your remarks, Hopkins," said the exile, uneasily.

"That all depends on you," retorted Hopkins. "Despite your croakings and fears, the first step we have taken has proven justifiable. We have accomplished what we set out to accomplish. I am invited to meet the fiend. Score one point for us. Now, when I advance a proposition for the scoring of a second point, you sneer. Well, sneer. I'll win the case for you, just to spite you. This despised note posted to Barncastle, I shall order a blue dress coat with brass buttons on it. I shall purchase, if it is to be found in London, one of those beaver hats on which the fur is knee deep, a red necktie, and a diamond stud. My trousers I shall have cut to fit the contour of my calves like a glove. I shall sport the largest silver watch to be found on the Strand, with a gold chain heavy enough to sustain a weight of five hundred pounds; in short, Chatford, you won't be able to distinguish me from one of Teniel's caricatures of Uncle Sam."

"You won't be able to deceive Barncastle that way. He's seen New Yorkers before."

"Barncastle doesn't know I'm a New Yorker, and he won't find it out. He thinks I'm from the Rocky Mountains, and he knows enough about geography to be aware that the Rocky Mountains aren't within two hours' walk of Manhattan Island. He knows that there is a vast difference between a London gentleman and a son of the soil of Yorkshire, and he doesn't know but what there are a million citizens of our great republic who go about dressed up in fantastic garments similar to those I shall wear to his dinner. If he is surprised, his surprise will add to his interest, and materially contribute to the pleasure of those whom he invites to see the animal the untamed poet of the Rockies. See?"

"Yes, I see," said the exile. "But clothes won't make the illusion complete. You look too much like a gentleman; your manners are too polished. A man like Barncastle will see through you in a minute."

"Again, Chatford, I am sorry that your possessions are nil, for I would like to wager you that your noble other self will do nothing of the sort. I have not been an amateur actor for nothing, and as for manners I can be as bad mannered as any nabob in creation if I try. Don't you worry on that score."

The acceptance of Lord Barncastle's invitation was therefore sent as Hopkins wrote it, and the ensuing days were passed by the young lawyer in preparing the extraordinary dinner suit he had described to his anxious client, who could hardly be persuaded that in taking this step Toppleton was not committing a bit of egregious folly. He could not comprehend how Barncastle upon receipt of Hopkins' note could be anything but displeased at the familiarity of its tone. The idea of a common untitled mortal like Toppleton even assuming to be upon familiar terms with a member of the aristocracy, and especially one so high as Barncastle of Burningford, oppressed him. He would as soon expect an ordinary tradesman to slap the Prince of Wales on the back, and call him by one of his first names, without giving offence, as that Barncastle should tolerate Toppleton's behaviour, and he in consequence was fearful of the outcome.

Toppleton, on the other hand, went ahead

TOPPLETON MAKES A FAIR START. 193

with his extraordinary sartorial preparations, serenely confident that the events of the next few days would justify his course. The exile was relieved to find that the plan was of necessity modified, owing to Toppleton's inability to find a typical Uncle Sam beaver in London; but his relief was short-lived, for Hopkins immediately proceeded to remedy this defect by purchasing a green cotton umbrella, which, he said, was perhaps better than the hat as an evidence of eccentricity.

"If I cling to that umbrella all through dinner, Chatford," said Toppleton, with a twinkle in his eye, "preferring rather to part with life, honour, or virtue than lose sight of it, I will simply make an impression upon the minds of that assembled multitude that they'll not forget in a hurry."

"They'll think as I do," sighed the exile. "They'll think you are a craz—"

"What?" asked Toppleton, sharply.

"They'll think you are a genius," returned the exile humbly and quickly too, fearing lest Toppleton should take offence. " Have you—er—have you considered what Barncastle's servants will think of this strange performance? They won't let you into the house, in the first place," he added, to cover his retreat.

"I shall be admitted to the house by Barn-

o

castle himself; for I prophesy that his curiosity to meet this Rocky Mountain poet will be so great that he will be at the railway station to greet me in person. Besides," continued Toppleton, "why should I care what his servants think? I never had nor ever knew any one who had a servant whose thoughts were worth thinking. A servant who can think becomes in my country a servant of the people, not the lackey of the individual. Furthermore, I am after high game, and servants form no part of my plan. They are not in it. When I go out on a lion hunt I don't bother my head about or waste my ammunition upon beasts of burden. I am loaded to the muzzle for the purpose of bringing down Barncastle. If he can't be brought down without the humbling of his butler, why, then, his butler must bite the dust. If I become an object of suspicion to the flunkies, I shall not concern myself about it unless they become unpleasant, and if they become unpleasant I shall corrupt them. I'll buy every flunkey in the house, if it costs a five-pound note."

"Well, go your own gait," said the exile, not much impressed by Toppleton's discourse. "If you are not clapped into a lunatic asylum, I shall begin to believe that the age of miracles is still extant; not that *I* think you crazy, Hopkins, but these others do not know you as well as I do. For my part, I think that by going to Barncastle's as your own handsome, frank, open-hearted self, you will accomplish more than you will in this masquerade."

"Your flattery saves your cause," said Hopkins. "I cannot be indignant, as I ought, with a man who calls me handsome, frank, and open-hearted, but you must remember this :, in spite of your long absence from your body, you retain all the commonplace weakness of your quondam individuality. You would have me do the commonplace thing you yourself would have done thirty years ago. If there is a common, ordinary, uninteresting individual in the world, it is the handsome, frank, and open-hearted man. You find him everywhere—in hut and in palace, in village, town, and city. He is the man who goes through life unobserved, who gets his name in the paper three times in his lifetime, and always at somebody else's expense. Once when he is born, once when he marries, and once when he dies, and it is a paid advertisement, not an earned one, each time. The first is paid for by his parents, the second by his father-in-law, the third by his executors. People like him well enough, but no one ever cares enough about him to hate him. His conversation ranges from babies—if he has any himself—through the weather to politics. Beyond these subjects he has nothing to say, and he rarely dines out, save with the parson, the candidate, or the man who wants to get the best of him in a business transaction. He is an idol at home, a zero abroad. Nobody is interested in him, and he would as likely be found dining with the Khedive of Egypt as with Lord Barncastle, and I'll wager that, even if he should in some mysterious manner receive an invitation to lend his gracious presence to the Barncastle board, he would be as little in evidence as an object of interest as the scullery-maid. Were I to accept your advice, Chatford, Barncastle's guests would be bored, Barncastle himself would be disappointed, and your chance of ever becoming the animating spirit of your own body would correspondingly diminish. Only by a bold stroke is success to be obtained. The means I am about adopting are revolting to me as a man of taste, but for the sake of our cause I am willing to stifle my natural desire to appear as a gentleman, to sink my true individuality, and to go as a freak."

"But why do you think you will succeed, Hopkins? Even granting that you make a first-class freak, has it really ever happened that idiocy—I say idiocy here not to imply that I think you are an idiot, understand me—has it ever happened that a freak succeeds with us where that better, truer standard which is represented by you as you really are has failed?"

"Not exactly that way," replied Hopkins. "But this has happened. Your Englishmen have flocked by the tens of thousands to see, and have been interested by an American Wild West show, where tens of hundreds have straggled in to witness the thoughtful Shakespearian productions of our most intellectual tragedians. Barncastle can have a refined, quiet, gentlemanly appearing person at his table three hundred and sixty-five times a year. He can get what I am going to give him but once in a lifetime, so say no more about it. I am set in my determination to stand or fall in the manner I have indicated."

"All right," said the exile. "I've nothing more to say; but there's one thing mighty certain. I'm going with you. I want to witness your triumph."

"Very well," said Toppleton. "Come along. But if you do, leave that infernal whistle of yours home, or there'll be trouble."

"I'm hardly anything else but a whistle. I can't help whistling, you know."

"Then there are only two things to be done. You must either get yourself set to the tune of Yankee Doodle, or stay right here. I'm not going to have my plans upset by any such buoy like tootle-toot as you are when you get excited."

"Perhaps, on the whole, I'd better stay home."

"I think you had," said Toppleton. "You would be sure to whistle before we were out of the woods."

Hopkins and his invisible client had hardly finished this interview when the tailor's boy arrived, bringing with him the fantastic garments Hopkins had ordered, and almost simultaneously there came a second letter from Barncastle of Burningford, which set many of the exile's fears at rest, and gave Toppleton good reason to believe that for the first part of his plan all was plain sailing. Barncastle's note was very short, but it was a welcome one, for it acknowledged the receipt of Toppleton's "characteristically American acceptance to dine," and closed with an expression of Barncastle's hope that Hopkins would become one of his guests for the Christmas holidays at the Hall.

"See, there!" said Hopkins, triumphantly. "That is the way my plans work."

"You are a Napoleon!" ejaculated the exile.

"Not quite," returned Hopkins, drily. "I

won't have any Waterloo in mine; but say, Edward, let's try on our Uncle Sam's."

"Let's!" echoed the exile. "I am anxious to see how we look."

"There!" said Toppleton, ten minutes later, as he grasped the green cotton umbrella, and arrayed in the blue dress coat and red tie and other peculiar features of the costume he had adopted, stood awaiting the verdict of the exile.

"You look it, Toppleton; but I think there is one thing missing. Where is your chin whisker?"

"By Jove!" ejaculated Hopkins, with a gesture of impatience. "How could I forget that? And it's too late now, for if there is one thing a Yankee can't do, Chatford, it is to force a goatee inside of forty-eight hours. I'll have to cook up some explanation for that—lost it in an Indian fight in Fairmount Park, Philadelphia, or some equally plausible theory, eh?"

"I think that might work," said the exile, in an acquiescent mood since the receipt of Barncastle's second note.

"I thought you would," returned Hopkins. "The little detail that there aren't any Indians in Fairmount Park, Philadelphia, doesn't affect the result, of course. But tell me, Chatford, how do I look?"

"Like the very devil!" answered the exile with enthusiasm.

"Good," said Toppleton. "If I look like him I've got Barncastle down, for if the devil is not his twin brother, he is his master. In either event I shall be a *persona grata* at the court of Barncastle of Burningford."

CHAPTER XIII.

AT BARNCASTLE HALL.

TOPPLETON'S surmises as to Barncastle's method of receiving him appeared to be correct, for upon his arrival, green umbrella and carpet bag in hand, at the Fenwick Merton station he was met by no less a person than his host himself, who recognized him at once.

"I knew it was you," said Barncastle, as he held out his hand to grasp Toppleton's. "I knew it was you as soon as I saw you. Your carpet bag, and the fact that you are the only person on the train who travelled first class, were the infallible signs which guided me."

"And I knew you, Barncastle, the minute I saw you," said Hopkins, returning the compliment, "because you looked less like a lord than any man on the platform. How goes it, anyhow?"

The Englishman's countenance wore a puzzled expression as Toppleton put the question.

"How goes it?" he repeated slowly. "How goes what? The train?"

"Oh, no," laughed Hopkins. "How goes it is Rocky Mountain for how's things, all your family well, and your creditors easy?"

"Ah! I see," said Barncastle with a smile. "All is well with us, thank you. My daughter is awaiting your coming with very great interest; and as for my creditors, my dear sir, I am really uncertain as to whether I have any. My steward can tell you better than I how they feel."

"It's a great custom, ain't it?" said Hopkins with enthusiasm. "that of being dunned by proxy, eh? I wish we could work it out my way. If you don't ante up right off out in the Mountains, your grocer comes around and collects at the point of his gun, and if you pay him in promises, he gives you back your change in lead."

"Fancy!" said Barncastle. "How unpleasant it must be for the poor."

"Poor!" laughed Toppleton; "there's none of them in the Rockies. You don't get a chance to get poor in a country where boys throw nuggets at birds, and cats are removed from back-yard fences with silver boot-jacks. Ever been in the Rockies, Barncastle?"

"No," returned the lord, "I have not, but

if all you say is true, I should like to visit that section very much."

"True, Barncastle?" said Toppleton, bristling up. "Why, my dear lord, that if of yours would have dug your grave out near Pike's Peak."

"I meant no offence, my dear fellow," returned Barncastle, apologetically.

"No need to tell me that," said Toppleton, affably. "The fact that you still survive shows I knew it. What time is dinner? I'm ravenous."

"Eight o'clock," replied Lord Barncastle, looking at his watch. "It is now only three."

"Phew!" ejaculated Toppleton. "Five hours to wait!"

"I thought we might take a little drive around the country until six, and then we could return to the Hall and make ready for dinner," said Barncastle.

"That suits me," returned Toppleton. "But I wish you'd send that gentleman with the mutton-chop whiskers that drives your waggon to the lunch counter and get me a snack before we start."

"No," said Barncastle, ushering Toppleton into his dog-cart. We'll do better than that. We'll give up the drive until later. I take you directly to the Hall, and send a cold bird and a glass of wine to your apartment."

"Good!" ejaculated Toppleton, with a smack of the lips. "You must live pretty near as fine here as we do in our big hotels at home. They're the only other places I know where you can get your appetite satisfied at five minutes' notice."

Toppleton and his host then entered the carriage, and in a short time they reached the Hall—a magnificently substantial structure, with ivy-clad towers, great gables, large arched windows looking out upon seductive vistas, and an air of comfortable antiquity about it that moved Hopkins' tongue to an utterance somewhat at variance with his assumed character.

"How beautiful and quiet it all is," he said, gazing about him in undisguised admiration. "A home like this, my lord, ought to make a poet of a man. The very air is an inspiration."

Barncastle shrugged his shoulders and laughed; and had Toppleton not been looking in rapt silence out through the large bowed window at the end of the hall they had entered, along an avenue of substantial oak trees to the silver waters of the Barbundle at its other end, he might have seen a strange greenish light come into the eyes of his host, which would have worried him not a little. He did not see it, however, and in a moment he remembered his mission and the means he had adopted to bring it to a successful issue.

"It beats the deck!" he ejaculated, with a nervous glance at Barncastle, fearful lest his enthusiasm had led him to betray himself.

"I find it a pleasant home," said Barncastle, quietly, ushering him into a spacious and extremely comfortable room which Toppleton perceived in a moment was the library, at the other end of which was a large open fireplace, large enough to accommodate a small family,. within whose capacious depths three or four huge logs were blazing fiercely. Before the fire sat a stately young woman, about twenty-five years of age, who rose as the Lord of Burningford and his guest entered.

As she approached Toppleton would have given all he possessed to be rid of the abominable costume he had on; and when the young heiress of Burningford's eye rested upon the fearfully green cotton umbrella, he felt as if nothing would so have pleased his soul as the casting of that adjunct to an alleged Americanism into the fire; for Lady Alice was, if he could judge from appearances, a woman for whose good opinion any man might be willing to sacrifice immortality itself. But circumstances would not permit him to falter, and, despite the fact that it hurt his self-respect to do it, Hopkins remained true to the object he had in view.

"Alice, this is Mr. Toppleton. My daughter, Lady Alice Chatford, Mr. Toppleton," said Barncastle.

"Howdy," said Hopkins, making an awkward bow to Lady Alice. "She don't need her title to show she's a lady," he added, turning to Barncastle, who seemingly acquiesced in all that he said.

"My friend Toppleton, my dear," said Barncastle, "has paid me the compliment of travelling all the way from his home in the Rocky Mountains in the United States to see me. He is the author of that wonderful sonnet I showed you the other night."

"Yes, I remember," said Lady Alice, with a gracious smile, which won Toppleton's heart completely, "it was delightful. Lord Barncastle and I are great admirers of your genius, Mr. Toppleton, and we sincerely hope that we shall be able to make your stay with us here as pleasant for you as it is for us."

Again Hopkins would have disappeared through the floor had he been able to act upon the promptings of his own good taste. It made him feel unutterably small to think that he had come here, under the guise of an uncultivated, boorish clod with poetical tendencies, to work the overthrow of the genius of the house.

"Thank you," he said, his voice husky with emotion. "I had not expected so cordial a reception. In fact," he added, remembering his true position, "I had a bet of ten to one with a friend of mine who is doing the Lakes this afternoon that I'd get frozen stiff by a glance of your ladyship's eye. I'm mighty glad I've lost the bet."

"He has some courtliness beneath his unpolished exterior," said Lady Alice later, when recounting the first interview between them to some of her friends. "I quite forgave his boorishness when he said he was glad to lose his wager."

"Now, Mr. Toppleton," said his host, "if you care to go to your apartment I will see that you get what you want. Just leave your umbrella in the coat room, and let Parker take your bag up to your room."

"Thanks, Barncastle, old fellow," said the Rocky Mountain poet, "I'll go to my room gladly; but as for leaving that umbrella out of my sight, or transferring the handle of that carpet bag to any other hand than my own, I can't do it. They're my treasures, my lady," he added, turning to Lady Alice. "That bag and I have been inseparable companions for eight consecutive years, and as for the umbrella we haven't been parted for five. It's my protector and friend, and since it saved my life in a shooting scrape at the Papyrus Club dinner in Denver, I haven't wanted to let it get away from me."

"How odd he is," said Lady Alice a moment later to her father, Toppleton having gone to his room. "Are you sure he is not an impostor?"

"No, I'm not," returned Barncastle with a strange smile; "but I know he is not a thief. I fancy he is amusing, and I believe he will be a valuable acquisition to my circle of acquaintances. Have you heard from the Duchess of Bangletop?"

"Yes, she will be here. I told her you had a real American this time—not an imitation Englishman—a poet, and, as far as we could judge, a character who would surely become a worthy addition to her collection of oddities; a match, in fact, for her German worshipper of Napoleon and that other strange freak of nature she had at her last reception, the young Illinois widow who whistled the score of Parsifal."

"The duchess must have been pleased," said Barncastle with a laugh. "This Toppleton will prove a perfect godsend to her, for she has absolutely nothing that is *bizarre* for her next reception."

Toppleton, upstairs in a magnificently appointed chamber, from the windows of which were to be seen the most superb distances that he had ever imagined, was a prey alternately to misery and to joy. He felicitated himself upon the apparent success of his plan, while bemoaning his unhappy lot in having to keep his true self under in a society he felt himself capable of adorning, and to enter which he had always aspired.

"It's too late to back out now, though," he said. "If I were to strike my colours at this stage of the battle, I should deserve to be put in a cask and thrown into the Barbundle yonder. When I look about me and see all these magnificent acres, when I observe the sumptuous furnishing of this superb mansion, when I see unequalled treasures of art scattered in profusion about this castle, and then think of that poor devil of a Chatford roaming about the world without a piece of bric-a-brac to his name, or an acre, or a house, or bed, or chair, or table, of any kind, without even a body, it makes me mad. Here his body, the inferior part of man, the purely mortal section of his being, is living in affluence, while his immortal

P

soul is a very tramp, an outcast, a wanderer on the face of the earth. Barncastle, Barncastle, you are indeed a villain of the deepest—"

Here Toppleton paused, and looked apprehensively about him. He seemed to be conscious of an eye resting upon him. A chill seized upon his heart, and his breath came short and quick as it had done but once before when his invisible client first betrayed his presence in No. 17.

"I wonder if this is one of those beastly castles with secret doors in the wainscot and peep-holes in the pictures," he said nervously to himself. "It would be just like Barncastle to have that sort of a house, and of course nothing would please him better than to try a haunted chamber on me. The conjunction of a ghost and a Rocky Mountain poet would be great, but after my experience with Chatford, I don't believe there is a ghost in all creation that could frighten me. Nevertheless, I don't like being gazed at by an unseen eye. I'll have to investigate."

Then Toppleton investigated. He mounted chairs and tables to gaze into the stolid, unresponsive oil-painted faces of somebody's ancestry, he knew not whose. Not Barncastle's, he was sure, for Barncastle was an upstart. Nothing wrong could be found there. The eyes were absolutely proof against peeping Toms. Then he rolled the heavy bureau and several antique chests away from the massive oak wainscoting that ran about the room, eight feet in height and superbly carved. He tapped every panel with his knuckles, and found them all solid as a rock.

"No secret door in that," he said; and then for a second time he experienced that nervous sensation which comes to him who feels that he is watched, and as the sensation grew more and more intense and terrifying, an idea flashed across Toppleton's mind which heightened his anxiety.

"By Jove!" he said; "I wonder if I am going mad. Can it be that Chatford is an illusion, a fanciful creation of a weak mind? Am I become a prey to hallucinations, and if so, am I not in grave danger of my personal liberty here if Barncastle should discover my weakness?"

It was rather strange, indeed, that this had not occurred to Hopkins before. It was the natural explanation of his curious experience, and the sudden thought that he had foolishly lent himself to the impulses of a phantasm, and was carrying on a campaign of destruction against one of the world's most illustrious men, based solely upon a figment of a diseased imagination, was prostrating. He staggered to the side of a large tapestried easy-chair, and limp with fear, toppled over its broad arm into its capacious depths an almost nerveless mass of flesh and bones. He would have given worlds to be back in the land of the midnight sun, in New York, in London, anywhere but here in the house of Barncastle of Burningford, and he resolved then and there that he would return to London the first thing in the morning, place himself in the hands of a competent physician, and trifle with the creations of his fancy no more.

A prey to these disquieting reflections, Toppleton lay in the chair for at least an hour. The last rays of a setting sun trembled through the leaves of the tree that shaded the western side of the room, and darkness fell over all; and with the darkness there came into Toppleton's life an experience that scattered his fears of a moment since to the winds, and so tried and exercised his courage, that that fast fading quality gained a renewed strength for the fearful battle with a supernatural foe, in which he had, out of his goodness of heart, undertaken to engage.

A clock in the hall outside began to strike the hour of six in deep measured tones, that to Toppleton in his agitated state of mind was uncomfortably suggestive of the bell in Coleridge's line that "Knells us back to a world of death." At the last stroke of the hammer the tone seemed to become discordant, and in a frenzy of nervous despair Toppleton opened his eyes and sprang to his feet. As he did so, his whole being became palpitant with terror, for staring at him out of the darkness he perceived a small orb-like something whose hue was that of an emerald in combustion. He clapped his hands over his eyes for a moment, but that phosphorescent gleam penetrated them, and then he perceived that it was not an eye that rested upon him, but a ray of light shining through a small hole that had escaped his searching glance in the wainscoting. The relief of this discovery was so great that it gave him courage to investigate, and stepping lightly across the room, noiseless as a particle of dust, he climbed upon a chair and peeped through the aperture, though it nearly blinded him to do so. To shade his eyes from the blinding light, he again covered them with his hand, and again observed that its intensity was sufficient to pierce through the obstruction and dazzle his vision. The hand so softened the light, however, that he could see what there was on the other side of the wall, though it was far from being a pretty sight that met his gaze.

What he saw was a small oblong room in which there was no window, and, at first glance, no means of entrance or exit. It was high-ceiled like the room in which he stood, and, with the exception of a narrow couch covered with a black velvet robe, with a small pillow of the same material at the far end, the room was bare of furniture. There was no fire, no fixture of any kind, lamp or otherwise, from which illumination could come, and yet the room was brilliant with that same green light that Chatford had described to Hopkins at his office in the Temple. So dazzling was it, that for a moment Hopkins had difficulty in ascertaining just what there was in the apartment, but as he looked he became conscious of forms which grew more and more distinct as his eye accustomed itself to the light. On the couch in a moment appeared, rigid as in death, the body of Barncastle; the eyes lustreless and staring, the hands characterless and bluish even in the green light, the cheeks sunken and the massive forehead white and cold as marble. The sight chilled Toppleton to the marrow, and he averted his eyes from the horrible spectacle only to see one even more dreadful, for on the other side of the apartment, grinning fiendishly, the source of the wonderful light that flooded the room, he now perceived the fiend, making ready to assume once more the habiliments of mortality. He was stirring a potion, and, as Hopkins watched him, he began to whistle a combination of discords that went through Toppleton's ears like a knife.

The watcher became sick at heart. This was the frightful thing he had to cope with! So frightful was it that he tried to remove his eye from the peep-hole, and seek again the easy chair, when to his horror he found that he could not move. If his eye had in reality been glued to the aperture, he would not have found it more firmly fixed than it was at present. As he struggled to get away from the vision that was every moment being burned more and more indelibly into his mind, the fiend's fearful mirth increased, at the close of one of the paroxysms of which he lifted the cup in which the potion had been mixed to his lips, and quaffed its contents to the very dregs. As the last drop trickled down the fiend's throat, Hopkins was startled further to see the light growing dim, and then he noticed that the fiend was rapidly decreasing in size, shrinking slowly from a huge spectral presence into a hardly visible ball of green fire which rolled across the apartment to where the body lay; up the side of the couch to the pillow; along the pillow to that marble white forehead, where it paused. A tremor passed through the human frame lying prostrate there, and in a moment all was dark as night. The ball of fire had disappeared through the forehead, and a deep groan told Toppleton that the body of Barncastle was once more a living thing having the semblance of humanity. A moment later another light appeared in the apartment into which Toppleton still found himself compelled to gaze. This time the light was more natural, for it was the soft genial light of a lamp shining through a sliding panel at the other end of the room, through which the Lord of Burningford passed. It lasted but a moment, for as the defendant in this fearful case of Chatford *v.* Burningford passed into the room beyond, the slide flew back and all was black once more.

With the departure of Barncastle, Toppleton was able to withdraw from his uncomfortable position, and in less than a moment lay gasping in his chair.

"It is too real!" he moaned to himself. "Chatford did not deceive me. I am not the victim of hallucination. Alas! I wish I were."

A knock at the door put an end to his soliloquizing, and he was relieved to hear it. Here was something earthly at last. He flew from his chair across the room through the darkness to the door and threw it wide open.

"Come in," he cried, and Barncastle himself, still pale from the effects of the ordeal he had passed through, entered the room.

"I have come to see if there is anything I can do for you," he said pleasantly, touching an electric button which dissipated the darkness of the room by lighting a hundred lamps. "The Duchess of Bangletop has arrived and is anxious to meet you; but you look worn, Toppleton. You are not ill, I hope?"

"No," stammered Toppleton, slightly overcome by Barncastle's coolness and affability, "but I—I've been taking a nap and I've had the—the most horrible dream I ever had."

"Which was?"

"That I—ah—why, that I was writing an obituary poem on—"

"Me?" queried Barncastle, calmly.

"No," said Toppleton. "On myself."

CHAPTER XIV.

THE DINNER AND ITS RESULT.

A HALF-HOUR later Toppleton entered the drawing room of Barncastle Hall, umbrella in one hand, carpet-bag in the other; his red necktie arranged grotesquely about his neck, the picture of Americanism "as she is drawn" by British cartoonists. Any other than a well-bred English gathering would have received him with hilarious enthusiasm, and Hopkins was rather staggered as he passed through the doorway to note the evident interest, and yet utter lack of surprise, which his appearance inspired in those who had been bidden to the feast to meet him. He perceived at once that he no more than fulfilled the expectations of these highly cultivated people, and it was with difficulty that he repressed the mirth which was madly endeavouring to take possession of his whole system.

The only portions of his make-up that

attracted special attention—if he could judge from a whispered comment or two that reached his ears, and the glances directed toward them by the Duchess of Bangletop and the daughters of the Earl of Whiskerberry—were the carpet-bag and the umbrella. The blue dress coat and tight-fitting trousers were taken as a matter of course. The red necktie and diamond stud were assumed to be the proper thing in Rocky Mountain society, but the bag and umbrella seemed to strike the English mind as a case of Ossa piled upon Pelion.

"Good evening, ladies," said Hopkins with a bow which was graceful in spite of his efforts to make it awkward. "I hope I haven't increased anybody's appetite uncomfortably by being late. This watch of mine is set to Rocky Mountain time, and it's a little unreliable in this climate."

"He's just the dear delightful creature I have been looking for for years and years," said the Duchess of Bangletop to Lady Maude Whiskerberry.

"So very American," said Lady Cholmondely Persimmon, of Persimmon Towers—a well-preserved young noblewoman of eighteen or twenty social seasons.

"Duchess," said Barncastle, coming forward, "permit me to present to you my friend Hopkins Parkerberry Toppleton, the Poet Laureate of the Rocky Mountains."

"Howdy do, Duchess," said Toppleton, dropping his carpet-bag, and extending his hand to grasp that of the Duchess.

"So pleased," said the Duchess with a smile and an attempt at hauteur, which was hardly successful.

"Glad you're pleased," said Toppleton, "because that means we're both pleased."

"Lady Maude Whiskerberry, Mr. Toppleton. Lady Persimmon, Mr. Toppleton," said Barncastle, resuming the introductions after Toppleton had picked up the carpet-bag again and announced his readiness to meet the other ladies.

In a very short time Toppleton had been made acquainted with all in the room, and inasmuch as he seemed so taken with the Duchess of Bangletop, Lady Alice, who was a young woman of infinite tact, and not too rigidly bound by conventionality, relinquished her claim to the guest of the evening, and when dinner was announced, permitted Toppleton to escort the Duchess into the dining-room.

"Don't you think, my dear Mr. Toppleton," said the Duchess as the American offered her his arm, "don't you think you might—ah—leave your luggage here? It's rather awkward to carry an umbrella, a carpet-bag, and a Duchess into dinner all at once."

"Nothing is too awkward for an American, Duchess," said Toppleton. "Besides," he added in a stage whisper, "I don't dare leave these things out of my sight. Barncastle's butler looks all right, but I've lived in a country where confidence in your fellow-men is a heaven-born gift. I wasn't born with it, and there hasn't any of it been sent down since."

"Aren't you droll!" said the Duchess.

"If you say it I'll bet on it," said Toppleton, gallantly, as they entered the beautiful dining-room and took their allotted chairs, when Hopkins perceived, much to his delight, that Barncastle was almost the length of the table distant; that on one side of him was Lady Alice, and on the other the Duchess of Bangletop.

"These two women are both an inspiration in their way," he said to himself. "Lady Alice, even if she loves that monster of a father of hers, ought to be rescued from him. She will inspire me with courage, and this portly Duchess will help me to be outrageous enough in my deportment to satisfy the thirst of the most rabidly uninformed Englishman at the board for American unconventionality."

"Have you been in this country long?" asked

the Duchess, as Toppleton slid his umbrella and carpet-bag under his chair, and prepared to sit down.

"Yes, quite a time," said Toppleton. "Ten days."

"Indeed. As long as that?" said the Duchess. "You must have seen a great deal of England in that time."

"Yes, I have," said Hopkins. "I went out to see Shakespeare's house and his grave and all that. That's enough to last a lifetime; but it seems to me, Lord Barncastle, you don't give Shakespeare the mausoleum he ought to have. Out in the Rockies we'd have had a pile set up over him so high that you could sit on top of it and talk with St. Peter without lifting your voice."

"You are an admirer of Shakespeare, then, Mr. Toppleton?" said Barncastle with a look of undisguised admiration at Hopkins.

"Am I? Me? Well, I just guess I am," replied Toppleton. "If it hadn't been for William Shakespeare of Stratford-on-Avon, you'd never have heard of Hopkins P. Toppleton, of Blue-bird Gulch."

"How poetic! Blue-bird Gulch," simpered Lady Persimmon.

"He was your inspiration, Mr. Toppleton?" suggested Lady Alice with a gracious smile.

THE DINNER AND ITS RESULT. 223

"That's what he was," said Toppleton. "I might say he's my library. There's three volumes in my library all told. One's a fine thick book containing the total works of the bard of Avon; another is a complete concordance of the works of the same author; and the third is the complete works of Hopkins Parkerberry Toppleton, consisting of eighty-three poems, a table of contents, and a portrait in three colours of the author. I'd be glad to give you all a copy, ladies, but it's circulated by subscription only."

"I should so like to see the book," said Lady Maude Whiskerberry.

"I'd be mighty proud to show it to you," said Toppleton, "and if you and your father here, the earl, ever pass my way out there in the Rockies, just look me up and you shall see it. But Shakespeare was my guiding genius, Duchess. When I began to get those tired feelings that show a man he's either a poet or a victim to malaria, I began to look about and see who I'd better take as a model. I dawdled around for a year, reading some of Milton's things, but they didn't take me under the eighth rib, which with me is the rib of appreciation, so I bought a book called 'Household Poetry,' and I made up my mind that Shakespeare, taking him altogether, was my poet.

He was a little old-fangled in some things, but in the main he seemed to strike home, and I sent word to our bookseller to get me everything he wrote, and to count on me to take anything new of his that happened to be coming out."

"Not a costly matter that!" said the Earl of Whiskerberry with the suggestion of a sneer. He did not quite approve of this original.

"No, my dear Earl," replied Toppleton. "For you know Shakespeare is dead—though I didn't know it at the time, either. But I got the book, and I tell you it made a new man of me. 'Here' I said, 'is my model. I'll be like him, and if I succeed, H. P. T.'s name will be known for miles around.' And it was so. It was not a year before I had a poem of 600 lines printed in our county paper, and there wasn't a word in it that wasn't Shakespearean. I took good care of that, for when I had the poem written, I bought the concordance, and when I found that I had used a word that was not in the concordance, I took it out and used another that was."

"That's a very original idea, and, I think, a good one," said Lady Alice. "You are absolutely sure of your English if you do that; but wasn't it laborious, Mr. Toppleton?"

"It was at first, miss, but as I went along,

and began to use words over again it got easier and easier, and for the last fifteen pages of the poem I hardly had to look up on an average more than six words to a page."

"But poetry," put in Barncastle, half closing his eyes and gazing steadfastly at Hopkins as he did so, "poetry is more than verbiage. Did you become a student of nature?"

As Barncastle spoke, Toppleton's nerve weakened slightly, for it was the very question he had desired to have asked. It brought him to the point where his winning stroke was possible, and to feel that he was on the verge of the struggle was somewhat disquieting. His uneasiness was short-lived, for in a moment when he realized how eminently successful had been his every step so far, how everything had transpired even as he had foreseen it would, he gained confidence in himself and in his course.

"I did, Barncastle; particularly a student of human nature. I studied man. I endeavoured to learn what quality in man it was that made him great and what quality made him weak. I became an expert in a great many osophies and ologies that had never been heard of in the Rocky Mountains before," answered Toppleton, forgetting his assumed character under the excitement of the moment and speaking, flushed of face, with more vehemence than the occasion seemed to warrant. "And I venture to assert, sir, that there is no physiognomy in all creation that I cannot read, save possibly yours which baffles me. I read much in your face that I would rather not see there."

Barncastle flushed. The ladies toyed nervously with their fans. Lady Alice appeared slightly perturbed, and Hopkins grew pale. The Duchess of Bangletop alone was unmoved. Toppleton's heat was hardly what was expected on an occasion of this sort, but the duchess had made up her mind not to marvel at anything the guest of the evening might do, and she regarded his vehemence as quite pardonable inasmuch as it must be characteristic of an unadulterated Americanism.

"Fancy!" she said. "Do you mean to say, Mr. Toppleton, that you can tell by a face what sort of a life one has led; what his or her character has been, is, and is to be?"

"I do, Duchess," returned Toppleton. "Though for your comfort as well as for that of others at this table, let me add that I invariably keep what I see religiously to myself."

The humour of this rejoinder and the laughter which followed it cleared the atmosphere somewhat, but from the gravity of his host and the tense way in which Barncastle's eye was fastened upon him, Hopkins knew that his shaft as to the baffling qualities of Barncastle's face had struck home.

"You interest me," said the Earl, when the mirth of his guests had subsided. "I too have studied physiognomy, but I never observed that there was anything baffling about my own. I am really quite interested to know why you find it so."

"Because," said Toppleton nervously yet firmly, "because your face is not consistent with your record. Because you have achieved more than one could possibly read in or predict from your face."

"I always said that myself, Barncastle," said the duchess airily. "I've always said you didn't look like a great man."

"While acknowledging, Duchess, that I nevertheless am?" queried Barncastle with a smile.

"Well, moderately so, Barncastle, moderately so. Fact is," said the Duchess, "you can stir a multitude with your eloquence; you can write a novel that so will absorb a school-girl that she can't take her eyes from its early pages to look into the back of the book and see how it is all going to turn out; you can talk a hostile parliament into doing violence to its secret convictions; but in some respects you are wanting. You are an atrocious horse-back rider, you never take a run with the hounds, and I must say I have seen times when you seemed to me to be literally too big for yourself."

"By Jove!" thought Toppleton. "What a clever fellow I am! If this duchess is so competent a reader of character as her estimate of Barncastle shows her to be, it's a marvel she hasn't found me out."

Barncastle laughed with a seeming heartiness at the duchess's remark, though to Toppleton, who was now watching him closely, he paled slightly.

"One of us is more than he expected, and two of us simply shock him," said Hopkins to himself.

"Of course, Mr. Toppleton," said Barncastle, "in view of my perfect willingness to have you do so, you can have no hesitation in telling me what you read in my face. Eh?"

"I have not," said Toppleton, gulping down a glass of wine to gain a little time as well as to stimulate his nerves. He had not expected to be so boldly met by his host. "I have not; but truly, my dear Barncastle, I'd rather not, for it's a mighty poor verdict that the lines of your face return for you, and inasmuch as that verdict is utterly opposed to your record, it seems hardly worth—"

"Oh, do tell it us, Mr. Toppleton," put in

Lady Alice. "It will be the more interesting coming from one who has so admired my father that he has travelled thousand of miles to see him. Do go on."

Hopkins blushed, hesitated a minute and then began.

"Very well," he said, "let it be as you say. My lord," he added, looking Barncastle straight in the eye, "if I were to judge you by the lines of your face, I should say that your character was essentially a weak one. That you possessed no single attribute of greatness. That your whole life was given over to an almost criminal tendency to avoid responsibility; to be found wanting at crises; to a desire, almost a genius I might say, for meeting your troubles in a half-hearted, compromising spirit which should have resulted in placing you in the ranks of the mediocre. The lines of your head are singularly slight for one of your years. There is hardly a furrow on your brow; on the contrary your flesh is so tightly drawn over your skull, that it would seem to suggest the presence in that skull of a brain too far developed for its prison; in other words your brain is as badly accommodated by your skull, I should judge, as a man of majestic proportions would be in the best Sunday suit of a little Lord Fauntleroy."

"You are giving me a fine idea of my personal appearance, my dear Toppleton," said Lord Barncastle, pouring a tablespoonful of wine into a small glass into which, if his guests had been watching his hands closely, they might have seen him place a small white powder.

"The strange part of it is that it is true, Barncastle," said the duchess. "I've thought pretty much the same thing many a time."

"Anything more, Toppleton?" queried Barncastle.

"Yes, one thing, my lord," said Hopkins, nerving himself up to the final stroke. "The eyes, one of our American poets has said, are the windows of the soul. Now if I were to look into your eyes at your soul, I'd say to myself, 'Hopkins, my boy, there's an old man living in a new house,' for I'll take my oath that *I* see the soul of a centenarian, Lord Barncastle, in the body of a man of sixty every time I look into your eyes."

Toppleton's bold words had hardly passed his lips when Lady Alice, who was becoming very uncomfortable because of the personal trend of the conversation, rose from her chair and gave the signal for the ladies to depart into the drawing-room, leaving Barncastle and his guests over their coffee and cigars.

"What an extraordinary gift that is of yours!" the Earl of Whiskerberry said to Toppleton as Barncastle walked with the duchess as far as the drawing-room door. "D'ye know, my deah sir, it's truly appalling to think you can do it, you know, because there's so much that—"

The earl's sentence was never finished, for a heavy fall interrupted him at this point, and Toppleton, turning to see whence it came, was horrified and yet not altogether displeased to see prostrate on the rug, white and lifeless as it had been in the room on the other side of the wainscoting upstairs two hours before, the body of Barncastle of Burningford.

"Frightened him out at the very first shot!" said Toppleton gleefully to himself. "He is easier game than I thought."

"I believe the man is dead!" said the earl, anxiously putting his hand over Barncastle's heart, and standing appalled to find that it had stopped beating.

"No," said Toppleton, with an effort at calmness, "this is a case of trance only—suspended animation. He will revive in a very short time, I fancy. This sort of thing is common among men of his peculiar character; I've seen it happen dozens of times. Have him carried to his room; tell Lady Alice that at my request he has started out to show me the Barbundle in the moonlight—in fact, say anything about me you please, only get up a plausible pretext for Barncastle's absence. I do not think his daughter knows he has these attacks, and there is no reason why she should know, because they are not dangerous."

With this the earl repaired to the drawing-room, where he made the excuses for Hopkins and Lord Barncastle. Toppleton and the butler carried the prostrate Barncastle up to his room, and then the American, utterly worn out with excitement, entered his own apartments to await developments.

CHAPTER XV.

BARNCASTLE CONFIDES IN HOPKINS.

TOPPLETON had not long to wait. His nerves had hardly resumed their normal condition when he heard a tottering step in the hall outside, followed by a soft tapping at the door.

"Who's there?" he cried.

"It is I, Toppleton—Barncastle. Let me in and be quick. I have something very important to say to you."

Hopkins ran to the door and opened it, and Barncastle entered, his face pale and his general aspect that of a man who had passed through a terrible ordeal.

"By Jove! I've landed my man!" said Toppleton to himself. Then he added aloud, "My dear Barncastle, you don't know what a turn you gave me downstairs. I sincerely hope you are not ill?"

"I am ill, Toppleton; ill almost unto death, and it is you who have made me so."

"I?" cried Hopkins, with well-feigned surprise. "I don't quite catch your drift."

"Your accursed faculty for reading character in the face, and searching out the soul of man in the depths of his eyes has made you the only man I have ever feared. We must come to some understanding in this matter. I want to know what your object is in coming here to expose me before my friends, to lay bare—"

"Object? What is my object?" returned Hopkins, with capital dissemblance. "Why, my dear fellow, what object could I have? I read your face and searched your eyes for indications of your character at your own request, and with your permission made known what I saw there—for it is there, Barncastle, plain as any material object in this room."

"It is dreadful! dreadful!" said Barncastle, covering his eyes with his hands and quivering with emotion and fear. "I had no idea your power was so great. Do you suppose for an instant that had I known how unerringly accurate you are as a reader of mind and face, that I would ever have asked you to lay bare to those people—"

"Dear me, Barncastle," said Toppleton, rising and putting his hand on the other's shoulder in a caressing manner, "really you ought to lie down and rest. This thing will all pass off with a night's sleep. You—you don't seem to be quite yourself to-night. You mustn't mind what I have said."

"You do not know, Toppleton, you do not know. You have done that to-night which has shown me that a dreadful secret which I have carried locked in my breast for thirty years, is as easily to be wrested from me by you as my jewels by a house-breaker."

"But, my dear fellow," said Toppleton, his spirit growing with pride at his success in bringing down his game with so little effort, "I—I understand that this is only one of the exceptions to the rules which govern the mind-reader's art. I do not really believe, of course, that what I seem to see beneath the surface is actually there. I—"

"Do not try to deceive me, Mr. Toppleton," sobbed Barncastle. "I, too, am something of a reader of character, as I told you, and I know exactly what you believe and what you do not believe. Had I been in such a position at dinner as would have permitted me to look as deeply into your eyes as you looked into mine, I should not have asked you to divulge what you saw. In fact, Toppleton, as you have probably seen for yourself, I have all along under-estimated your abilities, which do not, I confess, show up as advantageously as they might. You Americans are a cleverer people than you appear to be, and you have a faculty of dissemblance that is baffling to us in the older world, who have acquired candour through our conceit. We are so conscious of our superiority and ultimate ability to gain the upper hand in all that we undertake, that we do not consider it necessary to cloak our real feelings. The whole world speaks of the Briton's brutal frankness, and speaks justly. We are candid often against our best interests. We are impulsively frank where you Americans are diplomatically reserved. It is this trait in my people that makes it difficult for our Government to find suitable diplomats to fill the various foreign missions that must be filled, while your Government finds it difficult to find missions for all the diplomats who must be provided for. We have to train our Ministers and Ambassadors in the hard school of experience, as *attachés* to legations, while you have only to go to your newspaper offices, to your great political organizations, or to your flourishing business concerns to find all the Envoys Extraordinary you need with a comfortable reserve force standing always ready to step into any shoes that death, advancement, or revulsion of popular sentiment may make vacant. You are a great people; greater far than you seem on the surface, and it is this fact, unheeded by me who should have known better, that deceived me. I judged you from the standpoint of your exterior; I saw that you were a character, but beyond the green umbrella and carpet-bag indications I failed to look, and I thought I might safely venture the act which has come so nearly to my undoing. I see you now as you are. I apologize for underrating your ability, and I say to you frankly, that I rejoice all the more greatly in your proffered friendship since I have come to see that it is an honour not lightly to be worn."

"My dear Barncastle," ejaculated Hopkins, breathless with wonder and pride. "I assure you that your words overwhelm me. Your kind heart, I fear, has led you into over-estimating my poor character as much as you claim to have under-estimated it. I am by no means all that—"

"Ah, Toppleton!" said Barncastle, "let us not waste words. I know you as you are at last, and you need cloak your real self from me no more. I feared for an instant that you might be my enemy, though why you should be I do not know, and to have you read my secret as though it were printed upon an open page before you, filled my soul with terror. You have found me out, but you do not and you cannot know what has brought me to this unless I tell you, and I must insist that you become acquainted with my story, that you may the better judge of my innocence in the matter. When I have told you this story, I wish to exact from you a promise never to reveal it, for once revealed it would be my ruin."

"I do not wish, my dear Barncastle," said Toppleton, burning with anxiety to hear the other's story, and yet desirous of appearing unconcerned in order that Barncastle might throw himself unreservedly in his hands. "I have no desire to pry into another man's secrets, to wrest unwilling confidences from any man. If I have discovered one of your secrets, I have done so unwittingly, and I do not wish you to feel that I am holding you up, to use one of our Western expressions, for confidences. Keep your secret if it is one you wish to hold inviolate. I shall never tell what I have seen or what you have said to me."

"You are a generous, high-minded person, Toppleton. A poet at soul and a gentleman as well; but you must hear my story, for it is my justification in your eyes, and that is as necessary to my happiness, now that I know you for the man you are, as justification in the eyes of the world would become were the world to suspect what you have seen. I did not mind any portion of what you said at the table to-night, Toppleton, until you delivered yourself of the opinion that the soul of a man of a hundred and more years was dwelling in this body of mine, a body many years younger. Mr. Toppleton, I do not want you to think me mad. I want you to believe me when I say that what you saw is absolutely a fact. My soul has lived precisely one hundred and twenty-six years, my body sixty-one!"

Toppleton's expression of surprise as Barncastle spoke would have done credit to a tragedian of the highest rank.

"Excuse me, Barncastle," he said, kindly. "I really think you'd better let me send for Lady Alice and have the family physician summoned. Your mind is somewhat affected."

"Come with me," said Barncastle, rising from his chair and leading Toppleton out through the door into and along the hallway until they reached his private apartment. "I want you on entering this room to swear never to divulge what you shall see within, for I shall prove the truth of my assertion respecting my soul before you leave it, and, Toppleton, the maintenance of my secret is a matter of life and death to me."

"Of course, my lord, I shall not tell anyone of this interview except for your good. It is truly painful to me, for in spite of your apparent clearness of head I cannot help feeling that the excitement of this evening, together with the responsibilities a man of your position must necessarily assume, have made you feverish and slightly delirious."

"I shall dispel all such ideas as that," said Barncastle, opening the door and ushering Hopkins into his room. "Pray be seated," he said, "and do not leave your seat until I request you to."

"I hear and obey," quoted Toppleton, his mind reverting to the Arabian Tales, the splendour of his surroundings and the generally uncanny quality of his experience reminding him forcibly of the land of the Genii.

"I am going to prove to you now," said Barncastle, "that what I have said about my soul is true. Excuse me for being absent from the room for just five minutes, and also pardon me if I extinguish the light here. Darkness is necessary to convince you that what I say is truth; and, above all, Toppleton, look to your nerves."

Barncastle suited his action to his words. He extinguished the light and disappeared. In five minutes, during which time Hopkins sat in the inky darkness alone trying to formulate a plan for future action, a panel in the wainscot was moved softly to one side and Toppleton found himself face to face with the fiend.

For a moment he was numb with fear, but when the green shadow moved toward him and spoke in soft insinuating tones and appeared to fear him quite as much as he feared it, his courage returned.

"What the deuce is this?" he cried, springing to his feet.

"I am the soul of Barncastle. Barncastle lies prostrate as in death in the den beyond the wall. I am also the soul of Horace Calderwood who died forty-five years ago at the age of eighty, whose body lies buried in the yard of Monckton Chapel, at Kennelly Manor, Kent."

"What is the meaning of it—how—how has it come that you—that you are here?" cried Hopkins, with well-feigned terror. "What awful power have you that you can leave your body and appear as you do now?"

"Calm yourself, Toppleton. There is no awful power about it," said the fiend. "It is a simple enough matter when you understand it. I am simply an immortal soul with mortal cravings. I love this world. It delights me to live in this sphere, and it is given to the soul to return here if it sees fit. That is what makes heaven heaven. The soul is free to do whatsoever it wills."

"But how is it," said Toppleton, "that this has never happened before?"

"It has happened before. It is happening all the time, only you mortals never find it out. You want instances? The soul of Macchiavelli returned to earth and entered the body of a Jew; result, Beaconsfield. The soul of Cæsar returned to earth and entered the body of a puny Corsican; result, Bonaparte. The soul of Horace returned to earth and entered the body of an English boy; therefore, Thackeray. The soul of Diogenes returned to earth and entered the body of another English boy; result, Thomas Carlyle. Six souls, those of Terence, Plato, Æsculapius, Cicero, Cæsar, Chaucer, combined and, returning to earth, took possession of the body of a wayward child of Warwickshire; whence, Shakespeare."

"And the real souls of these men?" cried Hopkins.

"Became a part of space, and still so remain. How else account for the evolution of genius? Did you ever know a genius in his infancy?"

"No; I can't say that I ever did," said Toppleton.

"Well, with very rare exceptions geniuses are the stupidest of babies, or, supposing that in youth they give great promise, the valedictorian of his college class ends his life oftener than not without distinction, a third-rate lawyer, perhaps a poor doctor, a prosy clergyman, or as Mrs.

Somebody's husband. The man who is graduated at the foot of his class has oftener won the laurels than he. How is it accounted for? How did Keats, son of a stableman, become the sweetest of our sonneteers? In your own country, how did Lincoln and Grant spring from nothing to greatness? Was the germ of greatness discoverable in them in their youth? Would the most reckless of prophets have dared assert that the heavy tanner's boy would become the immortal hero of the Wilderness, the saviour of the Republic, the uncrowned ruler of fifty millions of people even with a thousand years of life to live? I tell you, Toppleton, the mystery of this life is more mysterious than you think. There are things happening every minute of the day, every second of the minute, the knowledge of which would drive a mortal mind—that is, a mind which has never put on immortality by passing into the other world—to despair."

"But, Barncastle," said Hopkins, his knees growing weak and his blood running cold, this time in actual terror, "how comes it that I, a mortal, inspire you, an immortal, with fear, as you claim I have done?"

"There is a point beyond which an immortal mind cannot with safety indulge in mortal habiliments. Have you never observed how men of genius outlive their genius? Did Bonaparte die at the height of his glory? Did Grant die at the zenith of his power?"

"D'Israeli did."

"D'Israeli embodied Macchiavelli, and Macchiavelli made no mistakes. I have made a mistake. I have lived too long as Barncastle, and every day beyond the day on which I should have left this body has lessened my greatness, my power, until I am become as weak as though I had never put on immortality. It is my craving to be among men, that has been my weakening, if not my ruin. The love of contact with mankind is as strong with me as is the love of drink with others. I cannot give it up."

"And the poor soul whose place you took?" said Toppleton.

"Don't speak of him," said the fiend. "I have made his name a great one. I have suffered more than he in my efforts to lift his personality to a plane it would never have reached had he been left to go his own way, to occupy his own person. He is my debtor, Toppleton. I have no feelings of regret for him. I went to him in a spirit of fairness and honesty, and offered to make him a famous man. He declined ;the offer. I assumed the risk of compelling him, and after the first compulsion he was acquiescent but not candid. When Horace Calderwood died, and I, his soul, for the first time learned that it was possible for a spirit to return to earth and do these things, the idea of depriving a fellow-soul of material existence was repellent to me, and seemed not to be strictly honest. He should enjoy, it seemed to me, something more than the consciousness of his greatness. He should be permitted to taste *in propriâ personâ* the delights of fame. And I resolved that I would not do as these others before me had done, and drive the real spirit of my,—ah—well, call him my victim if you choose—I resolved that I would not drive the real spirit of my victim out into space, leaving him to sigh and bewail his unhappy estate throughout all eternity. My plan was to go shares. To assume possession only so far as was necessary to insure the winning of the laurel; to let the other return to his corporeal estate in hours of leisure. I should have continued of this mind until to-day had I not had the misfortune to select for my operations an uncandid person, who had no genius, save that for tearing down what I was up-building. It became necessary for me to exile him for ever to save him from himself. He had been made a great man, and had I deserted him he would have become a conspicuous failure; his name would have been disgraced in proportion to the greatness it had had thrust upon it, and the soul of that one would have lived a life of humiliation and misery. What I did was the humane thing. I exiled him from himself, and I have no regrets for having done so."

"Well, of course," said Toppleton, "you know more about it than I do, but it seems to me it's a mighty rough thing to condemn a soul to perpetual existence on this earth deprived of the only means which can put him in a position to enjoy that life. If you are not joking with me, Barncastle, and your present appearance is pretty good proof that you are not, it seems to me that you have been guilty of a wrong, although your reasons for believing that you have done right are worthy of consideration. It strikes me that an omniscient, such as you pretended to be, ought not to have been bothered by the lack of candour of a purely finite mind; and, after all, it was but a bit of superb conceit on your part to think that you could do things differently from those who had gone before you."

"But my motive, Toppleton. Credit me with a proper motive," pleaded the fiend.

"Yes, I do," said Hopkins. "But out in the Rocky Mountains, my lord, we have lynched several thieves who stole to keep their families from starving. Their motives were all right, but they were suspended just the same. But let me ask you one question. To what extent do you retain that remarkable omniscient quality? I want to know, for candidly, much as I admire you, Barncastle, it rather awes me to think that you can penetrate to the innermost recesses of my brain—"

"I can no longer do that," said Barncastle. "My power through long confinement to mortal habitations has materially lessened, as I have already told you. Do you suppose, my dear sir, that, were it not so, I should be here, at this moment, unbosoming myself to you, and begging you in the name of humanity never to utter one word of what has passed between us? Do you think that I, who was once able to destroy a mortal's reason by one glance of my eye, would be so overcome by the words of a mind-reading American poet if I still had the power to subject his will to mine?"

"No one would believe me were I to tell him your horrible secret," said Hopkins. "Indeed, I don't know that I believe it myself. There is, of course plenty of evidence of which I have had ocular demonstration, but this may be all a dream. I may wake up to-morrow and find myself in my hammock in Blue-bird Gulch."

"No, it is no dream," said the fiend. "It is

all too real, but you will not expose me, Toppleton. There are those who would believe it, some who half suspect me even now would gain re-enforcement in their suspicions. My daughter would be shocked beyond expression and—"

"That, my lord," said Hopkins "is your convincing argument. Lady Alice's peace of mind must be held inviolate, and I shall be dumb; but I think you might let the exiled spirit enter once more into bodily life. The allotted days of the body you have wrested from him must be growing few in number. Why not atone for the past by admitting him once more?"

"There are two reasons, Toppleton," said Barncastle, fixing his eye with great intensity upon Hopkins, who maintained his composure with great difficulty. "In the first place, there are responsibilities which still devolve upon the Lord of Burningford which he would be utterly unable to assume. You might assume them, for you are a clever man. You have the making of a brilliant man in you, but he has not, and never will have. He is the most pusillanimous soul in the universe, and with him in charge, that body would die in less than six months. In the second place I have lost sight of him of late years, or rather lost consciousness of him, for he has been visible at no time since he departed from his normal condition, and since the day of my marriage, whose happiness he made a mad public endeavour to destroy, I have had no dealings with him. Where he is now, I have not the slightest idea."

"Well, I know!" ejaculated Toppleton, forgetting himself and throwing caution to the winds.

"You know what? Where he is?" returned the fiend, with a look that restored Toppleton's senses and showed him that he had made a mistake.

"Oh, no!" he replied, his face getting red with confusion. "Oh, no, not that. You interrupted me. I was going to say that I know—er—I know how difficult your—er—your position is in the matter, and—er—that I hardly knew what to advise."

"Ah!" returned the fiend, with a smile that to Toppleton's eyes betokened relief. "You have taken a load off my mind. Do you know, my dear fellow, that for one instant I half believed that you really knew of the original Chatford's whereabouts, and that perhaps you were in league with him against me. I see, however, how unfounded the impression was."

"How could you suspect me of that?" said Toppleton, reproachfully, his heart beating wildly at the narrowness of the escape. "But you don't intend to let him back?"

"Not if I can help myself, Toppleton," said the fiend. "I shall hang on here as long as I can, not only for my own sake and for that of my daughter, but also for the peace of mind of the exiled soul. You will respect my confidence, will you not?"

"I shall, Barncastle. You may count on me," said Toppleton.

"Good. Now I will resume the mortal habitation for which I have so long been a trustee, and we can rejoin the ladies."

Ten minutes later Barncastle and the Poet of the Rockies entered the drawing-room.

"Did you enjoy your walk, Mr. Toppleton?" queried Lady Alice.

"Well, I guess!" returned Toppleton. "Your father has one of the finest estates I have ever seen since I left Colorado, and as for your moon, it fairly out-moons any moon I've seen in the Rockies in all my life."

"It's the same moon that everybody else has," said the Duchess of Bangletop with a smile.

"Yes, Duchess," returned Toppleton, sitting beside her. "But you've furnished it better than we have. That Barbundle River gives it a setting beside which the creek in Blue-bird Gulch is as a plate-glass window to a sea of diamonds."

CHAPTER XVI.

MR. HOPKINS TOPPLETON MAKES A DISCOVERY.

It is hardly to be wondered at that Toppleton did not sleep much that night at Barncastle Hall. The state of his nerves was not calculated to permit him to sleep even had he been willing to do so. The experiences of the day were not of a nature to give him such confidence in his surroundings as would have enabled him to woo rest with a serene sense of safety. Furthermore, it was his desire to push his endeavour through to as immediate a conclusion as was possible, and time was too precious to waste in rest. Hence it was that the dawning of another day found him utterly fagged out, awake, and still meditating upon the means most likely to crown his efforts with success.

"I am afraid," he said, as he turned the matter over and over in his mind, "I am afraid it's going to be a harder task than I thought. My plan has worked admirably up to a certain point, but there it has ceased to result as I had anticipated. He is frightened, that is certain; but he cannot be frightened into a restitution. He is too selfish to give up Chatford's body and take his chances of getting another, and his rather natural distrust of Chatford's ability to sustain the greatness of the name of Barncastle re-enforces his selfishness. I can't blame him either. I haven't a doubt that Chatford's spirit would prove too weak to keep the body going a year at the outside, and yet it is his, and he ought to have it. He ought to—have—"

Here wearied Nature asserted herself, and Hopkins' head dropped back on the soft cushion of his couch, and he lost consciousness in a sleep that knew no dreams.

The morning hours passed away and still he slept. Afternoon gave place to night, and as the moon rose over the Barbundle and bathed the beautiful scene as with silver, Hopkins opened his eyes again and looked about him. He was annoyed to find that his vision had in some manner become slightly obscured; he seemed to see everything through a faint suggestion of a haze, and an object ten feet distant that he remembered admiring as he lay on his couch the afternoon before, its every detail clear cut and distinct to the eye, was now a confused jumble of lines only, suggestive of nothing in particular, though the moonlight streaming in through the window shone directly upon it.

"Dear me!" he said, passing his hands over his eyes as if to sweep away the filmy web that interfered with his sight. "I seem to have a slight vertigo, and yet I cannot understand why I should. I hardly drank anything last night, and as for what I ate it was simplicity itself. But I wonder how long I have been asleep; let me see." Here he consulted his watch, the great silver timepiece he had brought with him.

"Humph," he said; "half-past seven. I must have slept nearly thirteen hours; unlucky number that. No wonder I have vertigo."

He rose from the couch and walked, or rather tottered, to the window to look out upon the beautifully serene Barbundle.

"Mercy! How weak I am!" he cried, grasping the sill for support. "This trouble seems to have gone to my knees as well. I can hardly stand, and—ow—there is a touch of rheumatism in my right arm! I shall have to ring for Parker to bring me a little resolution in the form of a stiff horn of whiskey. These old English homes I'm afraid are a little damp."

He touched the bell at the side of the doorway and staggered back to the couch, falling upon it in a heap in sheer weakness, and as he did so he again became conscious of someone gazing at him from the other side of the room, and as he looked, the fiend in his emerald disembodiment took shape and approached him.

"Ah, Barncastle," said Toppleton, to whom custom had rendered the fiend's appearance less terrible. "I am glad to see you. I'm afraid I am ill. I have the most unaccountable weakness in my knees. My eyesight seems to have grown dim, and I am conscious of my head which is really a new sensation to me. I wish you'd send your butler up here with some whiskey."

"All right, I'll send him," returned the fiend with, or so it seemed to Toppleton, a lack of friendly interest in his tone which rather surprised him, for Barncastle had hitherto been the quintessence of politeness. "I fancy you'll be better in the morning; and between you and me I'd let whiskey alone. Brandy and soda is my drink, and I think it will do you more good in your present state than whiskey."

"Very well, Barncastle," Hopkins began.

"Don't call me Barncastle," returned the fiend, impatiently. "Your discovery of my secret has made all that intolerable to me, and I intend hereafter to spend as little of my time in that form as is consistent with propriety. I did not realize until you came here how long confinement within anatomical limits had weakened my powers, and to find myself at this period of my existence almost, if not quite, as incompetent to meet the grave crises of life as any mortal, is galling in the extreme. Call me anything you please, but drop Barncastle."

"Very well," again replied Toppleton. "I will call you my friend Greene."

"Humorous to the last, Toppleton," laughed the fiend. "That's a truly American characteristic. I believe you'll jest with your dying breath."

"Quite likely," said Hopkins, lightly. "That is if I ever draw it."

"Ah! Have you discovered an Elixir of Life, then?" queried the fiend.

"Not yet," returned Hopkins. "But I am sure I cannot see why, with your assistance, I should not do so. If you know all the secrets of the universe, I think you might confide at least one of them to me, and the only one I ask is, what shall I do to live for ever?"

"You are an insinuating young man," returned the fiend. "And I must say I like you, Toppleton, in spite of your abominable poetry, for now I am going to be candid with you."

"So much, then, is gained," said Hopkins, cheerfully. "If you like me, give me the recipe of life."

"I would, my boy," the fiend replied with a harsh laugh, "I would do it gladly, if I hadn't forgotten it. Some day I shall take a day off from these mundane operations of mine, and return to the spirit vale and freshen up my formulæ. Then perhaps I can help you. But I have something very important to say to you, and if you will come with me to my own quarters I will say it. This room is too chilly for a spirit with nothing on."

Toppleton readily acquiesced. His other sensations had been so acute since his awakening, that he did not realize until the fiend spoke of the chill in the atmosphere that he was himself cold to the very marrow of his bones; that his blood seemed hardly to run in his veins, so congealed had it become. He followed the fiend, who led the way from Toppleton's room to Barncastle's own quarters, where a log fire blazed fiercely on the hearth. There was no other light than that of the fire in the room, and Hopkins was glad of it, his eyes were too weary for any illumination save the one which made the darkness in which he now sat even blacker than was natural.

"Lie down there on my bed, Toppleton," said the fiend. "Lie down and listen to me."

Toppleton obeyed, and gladly.

" You are a sick man," began the fiend, "though you may not know it. You have no more than an even chance of living beyond this night. If you do live until to-morrow morning I see no reason why you should not continue to do so for many years to come; in fact I confidently anticipate that such will be the case, but you have got to be careful."

" If you were not one of the supernatural element, Mr. Greene," said Toppleton, nervously tapping his fingers together, " I should be inclined to laugh at your notions respecting my health. A man of my habits and physique doesn't go to pieces after a single late supper, to be brought up standing at the doors of death uncertain as to whether he will be invited in or requested to move on, all in a single night."

" For an acute man you are an obtuse sort of a person," returned the fiend, gravely. " I do not mean that you are in immediate danger of physical collapse, though that will come shortly unless you take care of yourself. It is a worse than physical death that I refer to. You are on the verge of intellectual death, Toppleton. You need twenty-four hours of wakefulness to put you in an insane asylum, an incurable, hopelessly mad for the balance of your days. You remarked a moment since that you were

s

conscious of your head. By that you meant that you felt the weight of it, and it is a leaden weight unless my eyes deceive me. I have experienced it, and I know what it means."

Hopkins' face blanched as the fiend spoke. It was too easy for him to believe all that had been said; and why should it not be so, he asked himself. Here was a case of mortal arrayed in combat against a supernatural being, and in the nature of things it was a contest of the intellectuals and not one of the sort in which Toppleton's training would have made him an easy victor. In a bout at arms Barncastle would have been a prey to Toppleton with scarce an effort on the American's part, but mind for mind, the young lawyer was fighting against terrible odds. He had proven to a very considerable extent a winner, and yet his victory was quite as hollow as the victory of a trotting horse who has won only the preliminary heats and still has the final test to undergo; but to win even the trial heat was a great thing, and that his mind should be well-nigh used up was to have been expected. Realizing this, and realizing also that it was his defeated adversary who was advising him as to what was necessary to be done for the preservation of his sanity, he was quite overcome. He nearly fainted, in fact he would have done so had not the fiend seeing his condition applied restoratives to his head and feet, and poured between his open lips a concoction which made every drop of blood in his body glow as with health, which imparted strength to his weary limbs, and which seemed to clear his aching head with its magical potence.

"You have had a narrow escape, my dear fellow," said the fiend, as Hopkins revived. "If I hadn't saved you, you would have stepped over the line."

"You—are—very—very kind," murmured Hopkins, raising himself on his elbow and then dropping wearily back into the pillows again. "You place me under very deep obli—"

"Don't speak of that," said the fiend with a smile. "The obligation you have placed me under is still greater. But now, Toppleton, you must sleep, or you will be beyond all hope to-morrow."

"I will," said Toppleton, faintly, and then he closed his eyes and consciousness departed from him.

The fiend regarded him for a moment and turned away with a sigh.

"If I had had the good fortune to operate on you instead of upon Chatford," he said, "well, there'd have been a president of the United States in your family by this time, or, better still, a railway king with an amount of brains equal to the possessions of the best of them. Oh, well! he wasn't to be had, and I haven't done badly with Chatford."

With which reflection the fiend passed from the room, and left Toppleton breathing heavily in sleep.

When next Toppleton opened his eyes consciously to himself, he was lying on a great oak bed with a tapestry canopy over his head. The sun was streaming in through the broad mullioned windows. The world without was white with snow, the tall evergreens down by the now ice-covered Barbundle presenting the only vestige of green in sight.

"Ah!" he sighed, as he looked wearily out of the window. "We shall have a white Christmas after all, but," he added, gazing about him, "how the dickens did I ever come to be here, I wonder? In Barncastle's own room—oh, yes, I remember. I fell asleep here last night and I suppose he has—Hello!—Who's that?"

The last words were addressed to whomsoever it was that entered the room at the moment, for the door had opened and closed softly.

"It is I," came a soft, sweet voice, and before Hopkins had time to place it, Lady Alice entered the room.

"Good morning!" said Toppleton, slightly embarrassed at the unexpected appearance of his hostess.

"Good morning!" she replied, coming to his side and stroking his forehead lightly. "And I can say with all my heart, after these awful days of suspense, that it is a good morning. You have been very ill."

"Oh, it was nothing," said Hopkins, endeavouring to conceal his surprise at the way things were going. "Only a little headache and rackety feeling generally. It will pass off. Barncastle was very good to let me have his quarters."

Lady Alice's face took on a troubled look.

"How beautiful it is out," said Toppleton, turning his eyes toward the snow-clad landscape again. "I was just thinking that we should have a white Christmas after all."

"Why, my dear, Christmas is over by two weeks. You have been ill here for three weeks yesterday."

"What?" cried Toppleton. "I?"

"Why, certainly," said Lady Alice. "Of course, you didn't know it, but it is so. You haven't had a lucid moment in all that time."

A sudden fear clutched at Toppleton's heart.

"But—but tell me, have I—what do—what

have the doctors said—that I had lost my mind, was in danger of a living death; that—"

"Don't get so excited," returned Lady Alice, softly, still retaining the look of anxiety on her face. "Here, read this. It is a letter from your Rocky Mountain friend, I think, and I fancy it will amuse you. It has only just come."

"My Rocky Mountain friend!" ejaculated Hopkins under his breath. "What devilish complication does this mean, I wonder?"

"Shall I open it for you?" asked Lady Alice.

"Yes," said Hopkins mechanically; "I'll be very much obliged to you if you will do so. Thank you," he added, staring wildly at the foot of the bed as the young woman opened and handed him the letter.

"While you are reading it," said she, "I'll run downstairs a moment, and tell Parker to prepare you a little breakfast."

"You are very kind," said Toppleton, faintly; and then as Lady Alice went softly from the room he began to read the letter. "'17, The Temple, London, January 2nd. My dear Barncastle—' Why, she must have made a mistake," he said; "this is for Barn—by Jove! it's in my handwriting, and signed—Hopkins—Top—ple—ton. What in the name of Heav—"

TOPPLETON MAKES A DISCOVERY. 263

Here he ceased his soliloquizing and began to read the letter which was as follows :—

"'My dear Barncastle,—I understood your game from the beginning. It was audacious, but unavailing, as the attack of a finite upon an infinite mind must always be. I led you on to your own undoing if you so regard it. I removed gladly every obstacle from your path, and let you think in your own conceit that you were an easy victor in the fight. By so doing I put your caution asleep, and when your caution slept you became a victim to my ambition just as did Chatford, with this exception, that I have left you in a position to enjoy life, while circumstances made it necessary for me to place him in perpetual exile. Perhaps when you get this letter and realize what I have done, you will curse me. Do not do so. You are not a loser in the premises. You have gained the Burningford estates, you have gained the enjoyment of the honours which I have won, at the expense of the difference of strength between the body I have put off and this one of yours which I now occupy. The latter, let me say to you, is a superb specimen, the ideal habitation for a soul like mine. Aided by it a still greater future than the one, to be paradoxical, I have left behind me, will be mine, and not mine only, but yours also, since it is under your name that my future greatness is to be achieved. I repeat, do not curse me, for in cursing me you but curse yourself, and when you get over the first sensation of horror at the changes I have wrought in our respective destinies, and can think upon it calmly and dispassionately, you will not find me so much to blame. Nor are you to be deprived of any of your years by my act. The infusion of a younger spirit into the corse of Barncastle will make it young again, and gradually you will recover the physical ground you now seem to have lost.

"I sail for New York on the *City of Paris* to-morrow, and you may rest assured that the name that now flies at the mast-head in the firm of Toppleton, Morley, Bronson, Mawson, Perkins, Harkins, Smithers and Hicks will no longer be a mere figurehead, a minimum among maxima; it will become once more what it used to be, a tower of strength in the legal profession, and, permit me to say, a tower of such height that beside it the famous structure erected by your illustrious father will become but as an ant hill to the pyramid of Cheops.

"Good-bye, Barncastle, for that is now your name. In the years to come we may meet again, and when we do, may it be in friendship, for as Barncastle I loved myself, and as Toppleton I love you. May you go and do likewise, and above all, give up masquerading as a Broncho poet, and get down to the business for which you were fitted by nature, if not by birth : that of a member of the noblest aristocracy in the world ; that of a peer of the British realm.

"Faithfully yours,
"HOPKINS TOPPLETON, *alias* BARNCASTLE,
"*Né* CALDERWOOD.

"P.S.—I have had an interview with the original Chatford, and have informed him that it is impossible for him to return to his former corporeal state, because Barncastle no longer knows the formula by which the re-entrance can be effected, which is true. He believes it, and has gone off into space with his whistle and his sigh."

For a moment Toppleton was overcome. This unexpected denouement was almost too much for him, but the indignation that surged up in his breast gave him strength to withstand the shock; and then, singular to relate, he laughed.

"To think that I should be born a Yankee and at my time of life become a peer surrounded by everything that wealth can procure, and loaded down with every honour that man can devise; oh, nonsense! it's all a joke, and a good one. Barncastle saw through my trick, and is paying me back in my own coin."

Here Hopkins laughed till the room echoed with his mirth, and as his laugh died away the door opened and the heiress of Burningford entered.

"Why, father!" she cried, exultantly, "do you feel as well—"

At the word "father," Hopkins' heart gave a great throb.

"My dear," he said in a moment, "I have

been ill you say for three weeks, and with no lucid intervals?"

"Yes."

"And my hallucination was what?"

"That you were that ridiculous American poet."

"Bring me the glass, my child," said Hopkins, gravely. "I—I'd just like to see my face in the mirror."

The glass was brought and Hopkins looked into it. The face of Barncastle in very truth gazed back at him from its silver depths.

"Ah!" he said. "I have changed; have I not?"

"Yes, indeed," said the Lady of Burningford. "But really I think your illness has done you good, for I do believe you look ten years younger."

"It is well," said the new Barncastle, with a sigh of resignation. "I have worked too hard. I shall now retire from public life and devote my remaining years to—to the accomplishment of my one great ambition."

"And what is that?" asked his daughter.

"To becoming a leader in the busy world of leisure, my child," said Toppleton, falling back to his pillow once more, and again losing consciousness in sleep.

This time fortunately the sleep was that of

one who had fought a good fight, had lost, but whose conscience was clear; and to whom, after many days, had been restored a sound mind in a body sound enough to last through many years of unremitting rest.

CHAPTER XVII.

EPILOGUE.

A SINGLE year has passed since the episode which brought our last chapter to a close.

The new Barncastle of Burningford is well and happy in the paths of pleasantness and peace, into which he was so unexpectedly and so unwittingly brought. His daughter has become engaged to a promising scion of a neighbouring house of large means and high estate in the social world. Hopkins Toppleton is in New York, busy at the practice of the law, developing a genius in the profession he had adopted for the convenience of his partners at which they stand amazed; steadily forging his way to the front, his energy, his aggressiveness, and extraordinary fertility of resource dazzling all beholders.

As for the weary spirit,—alas for him! He still whistles, wearily, through space, hopeless and forlorn, but at all times a welcome visitor to Burningford, whither he personally went, shortly after Toppleton's departure for New York, to lay his petition at the feet of Barncastle himself. He knows now what has happened to his young counsel, and his regret for himself is tempered by his regret for what he has brought upon him who so nobly undertook to champion his cause, for the quondam Toppleton has concealed from his first client the happiness that he feels over the strange metamorphosis in his fortunes, lest, comparing it with his own miserable condition, the exile may become more unhappy than ever.

THE END.

www.ingramcontent.com/pod-product-compliance
Lightning Source LLC
Chambersburg PA
CBHW031948230426
43672CB00010B/2085